Up the Airway

Note for Librarians: a cataloguing record for this book that includes Dewey Decimal Classification and U.S. Library of Congress numbers is available from the Library and Archives of Canada. The complete cataloging record can be obtained from their online database at:

www.collectionscanada.ca/amicus/index-e.html

ISBN 978-0-9781357-2-0

Printed in the Canada by Printorium Bookworks, Victoria, BC

Powell River Books
Powell River BC, Canada

Book sales online at:
www.powellriverbooks.com
phone: 604-483-1704
email: prbooks@shaw.ca

10 9 8 7 6 5 4 3 2 1

Up the Airway

Coastal British Columbia Stories

Wayne J. Lutz

2008
Powell River Books

Other Books by Wayne J. Lutz

Up the Lake
Up the Main
Up the Winter Trail
Up the Strait

To Wally...

Westview Flying Club's finest – a fellow aviator with a treasure of flying memories of the British Columbia coast

―――――――――――――――――

The stories are true, and the characters are real.
Some details are adjusted to protect the guilty.
All of the mistakes rest solidly with the author.

―――――――――――――――――

Front Cover Photo:
    Powell River, British Columbia
Back Cover Photos:
    Top – Aerial view 100 kilometres north of Powell River
    Bottom – Lac La Biche, Alberta

Acknowledgements

Writing is an easy process, when compared to editing. In return for the greatest editing any writer could ask, I offer my sincere thanks to Samantha Macintyre and Margy Lutz. In recent years, they have helped me overhaul my writing style, and this series of books is better because of it.

Interviews with many pilots have aided my efforts in this volume. Particular thanks go to Daniel Currie, Wally Berge, and John Randazzo. Members of the Westview Flying Club provided me with unlimited ideas regarding how to properly portray flying in coastal British Columbia.

Ed Maithus once again assisted with the artwork. When provided with the basic topic of an aviation cartoon, he navigates off in a direction that is always enlightening.

Throughout my writing projects, many Powell River businesses have stood behind my efforts. Three retailers have been especially steadfast in their support of my writing efforts and the marketing of my books, and they deserve special mention – Coles Bookstore, Marine Traders, and Breakwater Books. With friends like these, this series will continue to grow.

Wayne J. Lutz
Powell River, British Columbia
January 23, 2008

Contents

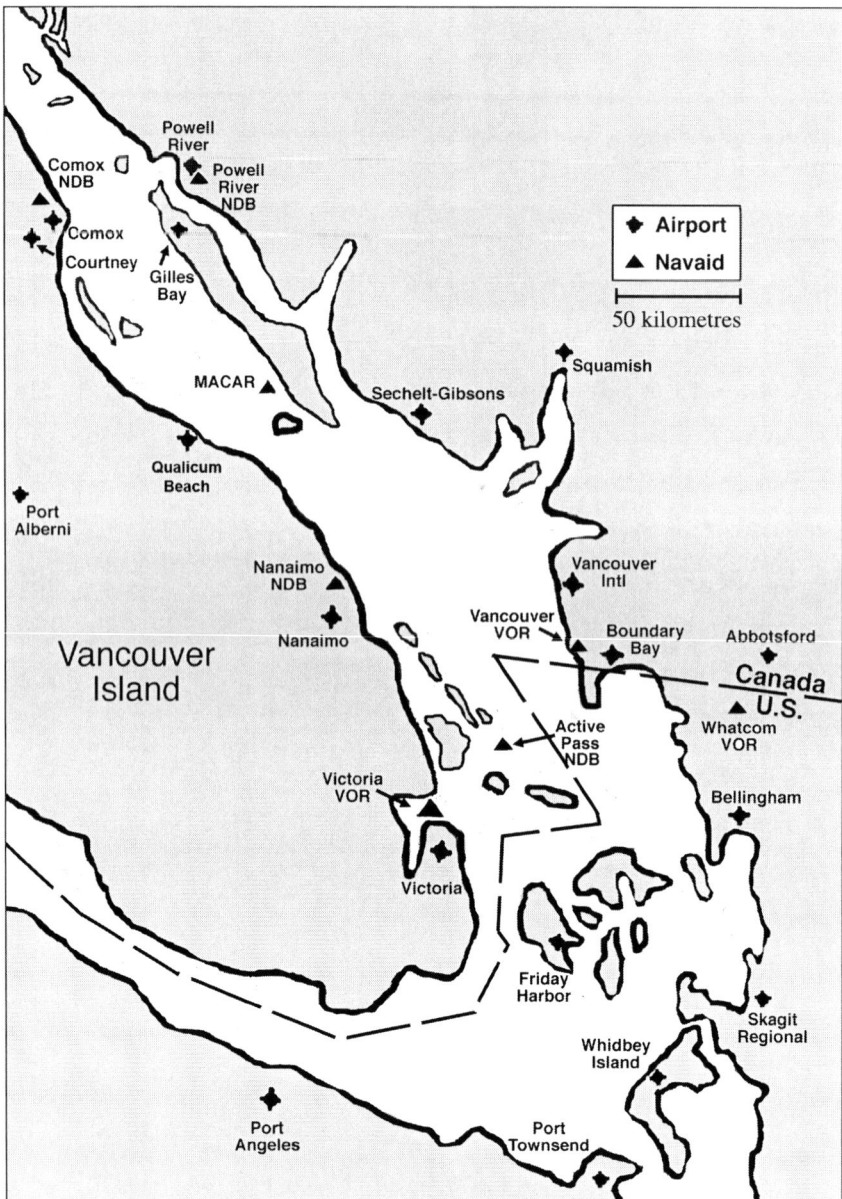

Powell
River

Comox
NDB

Powell
River
NDB

Comox
Courtney

Gilles
Bay

Airport

Navaid

50 kilometres

MACAR

Sechelt-Gibsons

Squamish

Qualicum
Beach

Port
Alberni

Nanaimo
NDB

Nanaimo

Vancouver
Intl

Vancouver
VOR

Boundary
Bay

Abbotsford

Canada
U.S.

Whatcom
VOR

Vancouver
Island

Active
Pass
NDB

Victoria
VOR

Bellingham

Victoria

Friday
Harbor

Skagit
Regional

Whidbey
Island

Port
Angeles

Port
Townsend

Airports and Navigational Aids
British Columbia South Coast & Northwest U.S.

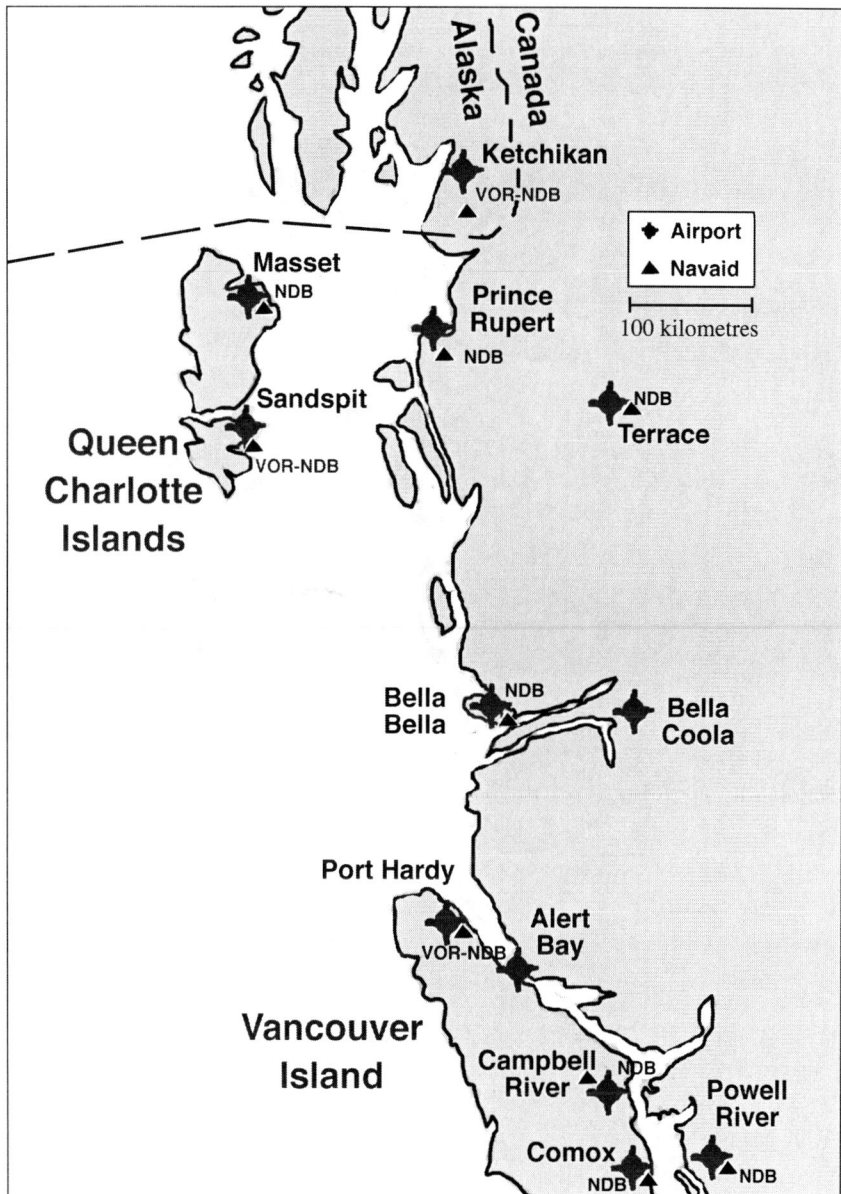

Airports and Navigational Aids
British Columbia North Coast

Canada
Alaska

Ketchikan
VOR-NDB

Masset
NDB

Prince
Rupert
NDB

Sandspit
VOR-NDB

NDB
Terrace

Queen
Charlotte
Islands

◆ Airport
▲ Navaid

⊢━━━━━━━━⊣
100 kilometres

Bella
Bella
NDB

Bella
Coola

Port Hardy

Alert
Bay
VOR-NDB

Vancouver
Island

Campbell
River
NDB

Powell
River

Comox
NDB
NDB

Mount Alice ✗

Olsen's Lake
Olsen's Landing ✗

Beartooth ✗

Emma Lake

Beartooth Creek

Clover Lake
Frog Pond
Goat Island

Goat Lake

Hole in the Wall

Powell Lake

Windsor Lake

Freda Lake

Tin Hat ✗

Mount Mahony ✗

Lewis Lake

Dodd Lake

Haslam Lake

Horseshoe Lake

E-Branch

Alpha Lake ✗

Knuckleheads ✗

Sliammon

Harwood Island

Powell River

Stillwater Main

Khartoum Lake

Westview Marina

Westview Airport

Duck Lake

Goat Main

Lois Lake

Rebecca

Hammil Lake

St. Vincent Bay

Ferries

Beach Gardens

Highway 101

Saltery Bay ✗

Ferry

Texada Isalnd

Malaspina Strait

Thunder Bay

Hardy Island

Nelson Island

0   5   10   15
Kilometres

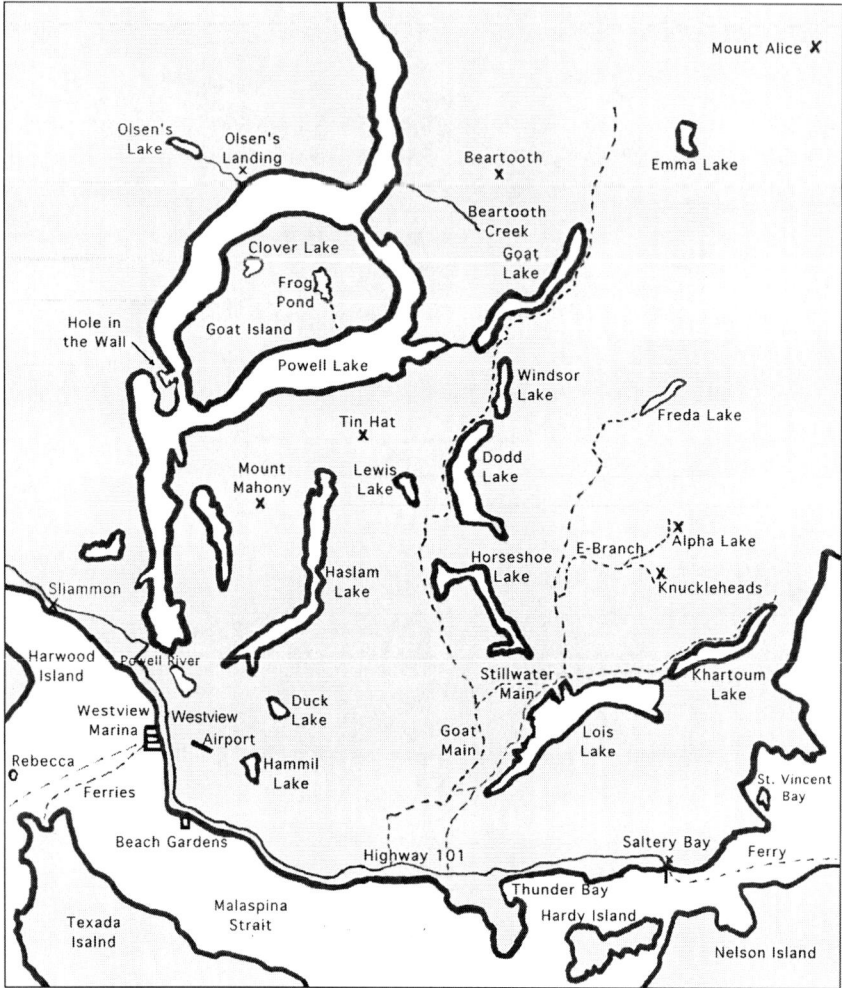

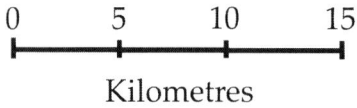

Powell River Region

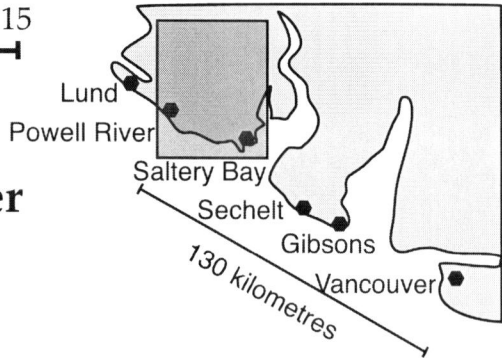

Lund
Powell River
Saltery Bay
Sechelt
Gibsons
Vancouver

130 kilometres

Preface

From the Cockpit

"Write what you know."

For decades I avoided giving in to this sage advice found in every introductory how-to book about writing. Instead, I turned my attention to science fiction and my series of books, *Coastal British Columbia Stories*.

Earlier in my writing career, I listened to the perceptive suggestions of experts, and tried writing about aviation, since it is certainly what I know best. But it didn't work. I've been ignoring the advice of such experts ever since. So too have I come to ignore those who offer publishing proverbs. The results haven't always worked out well, but it has kept me fiercely independent as an author.

When I turned to writing about aviation I immediately became bored. My boredom was not the result of the topic, for flying is my passion. But capturing a passion in words may be the most difficult task of all. Flying is just too beautiful, defying description.

Yet, even when not writing about aviation, I found bits of it sneaking into my chapters. In my science fiction writing, the protagonist flew a small airplane and the aliens faced C-130s (in a very indirect way). In my previous writing, my Piper Arrow serves as the backdrop in the scenes of several chapters. Aviation keeps side-slipping back into my writing. Maybe there's a bigger place for flying in my stories. And here it is – an entire book on the subject.

When I finally selected aviation as a subject for *Coastal BC Stories*, I faced an immediate problem. This first book about flying needs to fit into a series of stories that are read mostly by Canadians living on the west coast of British Columbia. Very few of these potential readers are pilots. Of course, I could abandon my regular readers in favor of pilots. But I won't!

Thus, the challenge – how to write about aviation in the context of coastal British Columbia, without losing my readers because of the details. Any book that hopes to capture the wonders of flight must remain true to the lingo, the equipment used, and the skills required by pilots. Aviation is highly specialized. Will my non-pilot readers be captured by the thrill of flying, just because I am? Answer: only if I approach the task carefully, with a flight instructor's attitude of taking things from the beginning, while letting the reader experience a few things by aerial immersion.

In this book about flying and coastal British Columbia, the airplane becomes a tool for finding the people and places that make this region extraordinary. But the high-tech equipment, aeronautical terminology, and the complexity of aviation itself have not been toned down just because the audience includes those who are not aviators. In fact, that is the real challenge – to draw the reader into the cockpit without the need for a background in aeronautics. Keeping it real, without glossing over the details.

The success or failure of my efforts will be determined by whether an audience of non-pilots wants to experience the thrills of flight. I think they do. In coastal BC, there are boaters, fishermen, loggers, and other self-reliant individuals – whole rural communities of independent people who are used to the challenges posed by remoteness. The airplane helps deal with such challenges, and they all know it. I believe these readers will enjoy flying as my copilot, occasionally taking over the controls themselves. I look forward to introducing them to the instruments, switches, and flight controls that will take us loft to unique destinations.

There is another oft-repeated saying in self-help books for authors: "Show, don't tell." It's a technique that will apply well to stories like these. So, take control of the aircraft. Rest your left hand on the yoke and your right hand on the throttle. Move your feet up over the rudder pedals. As we fly, keep an eye on the horizon, closely monitor altitude and airspeed, and cast a glance at the engine gauges. Let me show you how to fly.

And to those pilots who read this book, I say welcome aboard. You are an important part of this aircrew, although in an entirely different way. Together we'll share the thrill of cruising over glaciated peaks and past mountains that drop into the sea. We'll align our aircraft on the runway's narrow swath through the trees in a remote location and slide down the glide slope. Our passengers are going to love the ride.

◊ ◊ ◊ ◊ ◊ ◊

Chapter 1

Bella Bella

The maze of waterways stretches below, flowing onward into the mountains on both sides. By now I know a lot about this region. I've studied it on the map for years, but from aloft it looks different. How did mariners ever navigate through this jumble of islands and inlets without GPS? Without my cockpit navigational equipment, I'd be lost, even from an aerial perch that provides such an optimum view of the surrounding landmarks.

The patchy clouds below the Piper Arrow deter my efforts to maintain spatial orientation. Is that Bute Inlet? A stratocumulus layer covers Stuart Island and Ramsay Arm, and mighty Bute blends into the background of nearby fjords. Impressive inlets are rendered into river-like extensions.

Margy flies from the pilot's left seat, while I sit contentedly to her right. She controls the airplane, while I do what I enjoy the most – navigation and communication. We share the rewarding tasks of flight, enhanced by decades of flying together.

Over the years, we have developed areas of expertise, though either of us is capable of handling this airplane solo. Margy usually flies during takeoffs, providing me plenty of time to monitor the engine instruments during this critical phase. It also gives me an opportunity to attend to the navigation radios.

We use a challenge-and-response approach to each flight, a method that encourages each of us to check the assigned tasks of the other pilot. Sometimes, simple tasks can be mishandled when complacency and inattention creep into the cockpit. Margy might ask: "Is the GPS set up for our next leg?" Or I seek verification of the obvious: "Do you still have the floatplane in sight?" We've caught a lot of minor errors this way, things that could quickly compromise safety.

Today, I'm the one who contacts Flight Service on the enroute frequency, announcing our full call sign including the "November" prefix designating our airplane as U.S. registered. That's far from necessary, since the lack of continuous letters in the identification gives us away as Americans.

As soon as I establish contact, I state that we are on a "flight note," a visual cross-country procedure that is simpler than a standard flight plan. With our friend, John, as our "responsible party" back in Powell River, a flight notification is excellent insurance. If we don't check in with John by telephone on schedule, he'll promptly launch search and rescue through Flight Service. He also tracks us with his own "personal radar," in and out of areas where radio communication is nonexistent. You can't hide from John for long.

I ask Flight Service for the latest weather reports for Bella Bella and the status of the restricted area northeast of Port Hardy. There is no weather data from Bella Bella, but the female voice offers two recent lighthouse reports in the area. The conditions looks good (winds light, sea rippled), and the restricted area north of Port Hardy is not active, so we can cut the corner and join the airway that runs north to Bella Bella.

I push my seat back and settle in for the remaining hour of cruise flight. Margy has engaged the autopilot, and serenity pervades the cockpit. A Beaver on floats checks in on the Flight Service frequency. The floatplane is on a Nav Canada flight itinerary to the Queen Charlottes, a tracking notification procedure more relaxed than a complete flight plan, but more formal than a flight note.

On this mid-July day, a massive ridge of high pressure dominates the entire British Columbia central and south coast. The forecast calls for it to remain parked here for a while. It's one of those perfect days for flying.

Two kilometres below, isolated boats are tucked into inlets and sheltered bays, enjoying their own solitude far from the bustle of any city or town. From the water, the only sign of humanity is a tiny maroon and white airplane passing overhead, a faint engine droning high above. I doubt they even notice.

* * * * *

Eighty miles up the electronically defined airway from Port Hardy VOR, Margy turns the airplane's flight controls over to me. Still on autopilot, this is merely an acknowledgement, verifying who is in charge. When we are twenty miles from the airport, I push the knob on the autopilot's pitch trim to begin the descent into Bella Bella. The airspeed indicator winds up, and I pull back on the throttle just a little to keep the increased velocity under control.

I'm usually the one who flies the descent into the more exciting airports. We share the landings, but I get the flight controls at the most unusual airstrips. My flying hours exceed Margy's, and that shows up more in airport arrivals than in any other phase of flight. Margy handles landings in the Arrow well, but she doesn't possess the comfort level that more flight hours can deliver. So I fly more arrivals than departures, and the landings I get are sometimes exciting.

The stratus clouds beneath us are broken, with lots of opportunities to weave around them as we descend. I reach forward to disengage the autopilot switch, then waggle the wings to assure I have control.

"Want the landing tank now?" asks Margy.

"Sure. Move it over."

She reaches down next to her left foot, and switches the fuel selector from *Right* to *Left*, giving us the fullest tank for landing. It's one of the only switches that's difficult to reach from my side of the cockpit. As a flight instructor, I feel more comfortable in the right seat, yoke in my right hand, throttle in my left. It's my natural place.

There are two airports at Bella Bella. We descend over the Denny Island airstrip in a wide spiral, inspecting it as a prospective camping spot. It's more isolated than the primary airport on nearby Campbell Island. The Denny Island runway is wide with no taxiway, typical of Canadian airports. The parking area has no airplanes; a lone truck is parked near a white trailer that sits adjacent to the ramp.

We survey the dirt road that runs from the end of the runway to the bay. You get a good preview of the terrain from two thousand feet up, so we absorb as much of the detail as possible in preparation for travel once we're on the ground. It looks like an ideal spot to camp, but first we'll visit the other Bella Bella.

So I point the nose westward towards Campbell Island and the airfield that serves the First Nations village. This runway is significantly uphill to the northwest, and our landing will be almost directly into the wind. It should be a short uphill roll.

I turn base leg for Runway 31, right over the town. I fly the approach, while Margy surveys the road from the airport to the village, and decides how to walk to the harbour.

The pre-landing checklist is already complete, but I recite the final two items again: "Three green, prop full forward." The landing gear is down and locked, and the propeller is set to maximum RPM in anticipation of a possible go-around. It's a good rule of thumb to treat every landing like a potential missed approach.

The wind on short final includes a left crosswind component, as verified by a barely perceptible drift to the right. So I offer a little left aileron and enough right rudder to remain aligned with the runway's centerline. As we come in over the fence, I gradually pull back on the throttle, simultaneously easing the yoke rearward in the flare. The touchdown is abrupt, not gentle, but doesn't waste any runway – a good landing for a short strip. And the destination is typical of British Columbia – supernatural.

* * * * *

We hike down the road from the airport, a pleasant descent into the town on a relatively cool July day. We pass the dump, traditionally located adjacent to this semi-remote airport. Airport crows do double duty in such environments – dump scavengers and homing beacons to help us find our way back to the airplane after an off-airport hike.

Boats sit on the open ground on both sides of the road. Most are of metal construction, in sizes that range from small to huge – some derelict, but most are still serviceable. A few of these boats are in the middle of vacant lots, while others sit adjacent to houses. Many are flat on the ground, without trailers.

We pass a house with a small-scale basketball net abutting the paved road. On the other side of the road, another net stands ready at the neighbor's house; a complete basketball court on pavement. It's a good thing there are few vehicles. "Go play in the road" has a different meaning here.

As we continue down the street into the heart of town, some homes sport hand-lettered signs advertising: *Pop and Ice Cream* and *Videos*. The houses range from new, with modern wood design, to old and dilapidated. All have a gorgeous ocean view.

Another play area on the edge of the road has a small hockey net poised for action. Mom and dad are currently enjoying a hockey shoot-out contest with their young daughter who can barely maneuver the adult-size hockey stick. We walk through the middle of their rink as the girl whacks the fluorescent orange puck as best she can. The puck wobbles, momentarily gets up on its side, and rolls awkwardly towards the goal. Her shot is unblocked by the goalie (dad), and rolls into the net. I can't resist cheering her on.

"She shoots. She scores!" I yell.

This must be universal terminology, since dad smiles proudly back at me.

Both marinas are on the top of our must-see list, and we are not disappointed. Classic fishing boats geared for salmon are tucked in everywhere along the docks. Modern Honda outboards are the engine of choice here. The big shiny silver four-stroke outboards look out of place in this work environment, but they obviously do the job just fine. Many are mounted on flat-bottomed metal boats that could haul a mighty big catch.

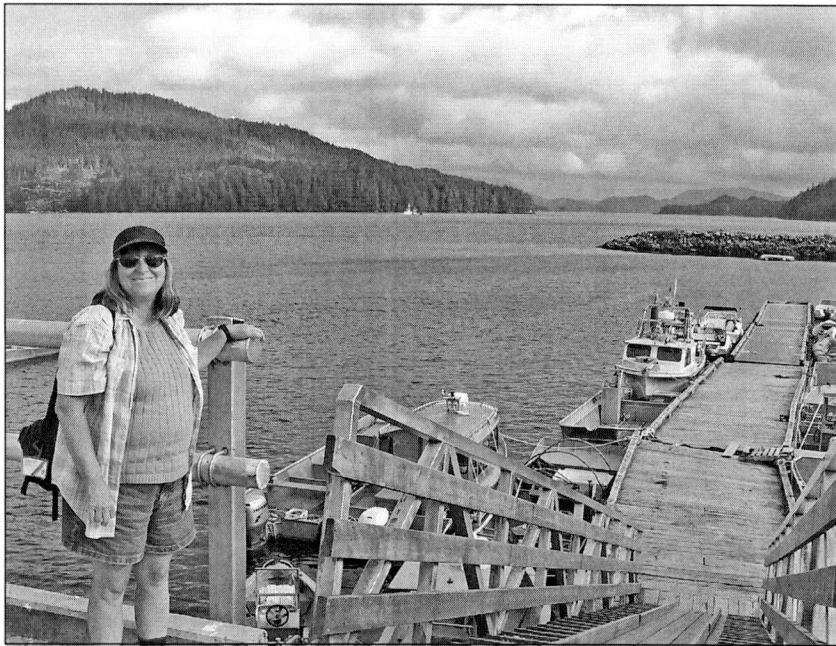

From the second dock, we look across to Denny Island, where an expansive new complex of subdued pastel buildings sit pristine and seemingly vacant. Could this be an extensive resort, a bit out of place here? I focus my binoculars on the buildings. In my mind, I equate what I see to a line of new townhouses.

"What are those buildings?" I ask the only other man on the dock. The young fellow has just arrived and is arranging the rigging on his fishing pole.

"New Fisheries place," replies the youth, not pausing his concentration as he sets up his line.

I interpret this as an uninterested reply from a man who has seen new government construction spread all around him.

"Pretty big for offices," I note. "Is it housing for the Fisheries workers too?"

"Not open yet," he replies. "Big government thing."

"Jobs for Canadians," I remark.

I succeed in getting a laughing grunt from the fisherman. It's one of my favorite phrases. From my perspective, it seems that many government jobs in BC serve few purposes except for creating make-work projects.

"But not for us," says the man in a disgusted monotone.

Even reluctant acceptance doesn't win any victories in a continual battle with the government.

Adjacent to this out-of-place symbol of government affluence are two old industrial buildings, dirty white but still standing strong and looking proud. They are separated from the new complex by several rows of trees.

"What about those white buildings to the left?" I ask.

"The old cannery, BC Packers. It's been closed a long time. There's another one up there that's still open." He sweeps his arm to the right. "Not much canning these days."

* * * * *

A local taxi is one of the best ways to learn about a town. But getting one is sometimes a challenge. The clerk in the First Nations co-op is glad to help, but her telephone calls to the cab driver go unanswered.

"No one is home," she says, offering no other alternative.

Two teenagers are clowning around in the front of the store, and I boldly step towards the youths, although they seem reluctant to meet my gaze.

"Would you be interested in earning some money by taking us for a tour of the island?"

"No car," says one of the boys.

I feel bad that I asked.

Part of the co-op is set aside as a cafe, so we ask the waitress for a suggestion.

"A taxi just picked up a dinner order," she says. "I'll call him back."

She dials a phone number, mumbles a few words, and hangs up.

"He's coming back for you."

The timing is perfect. Within seconds, an unmarked red van pulls up in front of the store's entrance, parking audaciously like a taxi with prestige.

"Can we hire you for a ride?" I inquire into the open passenger window.

The taxi driver is a rotund, smiling fellow who looks like he could tell a good story.

"Sure. Where do you want to go?"

"Eventually to the airport. But could you drive around the roads in the area first?"

"Okay, but that won't take long."

"Keep it under 100 kilometres," I joke, as we slip into the back seat with our backpacks.

"Make it about two klicks, and you've seen it all," he laughs.

This is a town of 1600 residents, an amazingly large population for a settlement of this physical size. Many of the homes include extended families that number into the double-digits.

"That's the RCMP building. Sixteen cops," says the taxi driver.

That's one policeman for every 100 people.

"The cops have the best houses," he says. "The hospital workers too. Want to see our bar? – it's one of the biggest on the west coast."

The bar is closed, and it's not very impressive looking. But it is big. Alcohol is allowed here, not a common occurrence in most First Nations villages.

"Almost all of our population is native," says the taxi driver. "Except for the police, teachers, and hospital workers. But we have some half-breeds. There used to be a military base on Denny Island, so you'll find lots of red-haired and green-eyed mixed race around here. These days, Denny Island has 400 people scattered throughout the island, with houses for lawyers, retired teachers, and others with wealth."

The taxi driver has some experience coordinating with other bands throughout the region, assisting them with the organization of their community services and finances. His primary job these days is driving heavy equipment.

"Most of the bands don't understand the importance of looking ahead," he says. "Take garbage, for instance. Bears and cougars are beginning to appear in the town. We've let the garbage dumps go too long."

We pull through a nicely landscaped cul-de-sac – homes for the cops. At the end of the road, a scraggly tan dog sits in the middle of the small turnaround area. Our van pirouettes around the dog, not slowing in the least as we reverse course. I look out my side window as we pivot around the dog, missing him by only a few inches. He continues to lie on the road with an eye on the van, but doesn't budge, and the cab driver doesn't even acknowledge his existence. I guess both dog and van are used to this maneuver.

Passing the school, we get a view of the nicely-manicured new athletic field and the teachers' homes on the slope above. We continue on to the small ferry dock that handles the traffic between Port Hardy and Prince Rupert.

"This is where we pack the salmon. Those pallets are where they ice 'em down."

"What about tourists?" I ask. "There's a lot of Pacific Coastal activity at the airport, but I haven't seen any tourists."

"That's another area where the elders haven't kept up," he notes. "The airlines bring in the sport fishermen to our island, and the fishing resort bosses wait off-shore in their boats to haul them away."

"You mean they just come in and take the tourists off the island as soon as they arrive."

"Yup. They make all of the money, and we get nothing. Boats are waiting out there right now."

Tourist poaching at its best. Bella Bella doesn't even receive any of the spoils.

* * * * *

Back at the airport, we sit in the van, talking for a few minutes more. It has been an ideal tour, just what we were hoping for.

"How much do we owe you?" asks Margy.

"Six dollars will do it," says the taxi driver.

Now there's a bargain price commensurate with a town that hasn't discovered tourism.

We give the driver twenty dollars and our sincere thanks. Then we slip through the opening in the gate that is designated for after-hours access. Not exactly tight airport security, but it works for us.

We plan to camp across the channel at the airport on Denny Island, which we surveyed from the air during our arrival. We are ready for takeoff in only a few minutes, back-taxiing to take advantage of the downhill slope on Runway 13. Engine run-up and magneto check complete, I position the aircraft on the end of the runway. We face downhill towards the town. About a half-mile off the end of the runway's far threshold, a microwave tower sticks up, directly aligned with the pavement's extended centerline. It's not a major obstacle (as long as you notice it's there), but it's an unusual placement. With all this open land, it seems strange for a major tower to be constructed right off the end of the runway. It would never meet government airport standards, but somehow it was built as if it was intentionally surveyed to line up with the runway.

Once airborne, I make an immediate left turn to clear the microwave tower and point the Arrow's nose towards Denny Island. It's not worth climbing above a thousand feet for the short flight, and within a few minutes we are entering the downwind leg for a landing. While I work through the arrival checklist, Margy gets a second look at the path down to the water from the airport, and hunts for the windsock. When she points out the cloth sock to me, I notice that it is wrapped around its pole, a worthless indicator of wind direction. My guess is that it has been out of commission for quite a while.

On final approach, I am a little concerned. Landing almost directly into the sun, the glare makes it hard to identify the runway features. Surely this short strip can't be as wide as it looks. The paved runway must be surrounded by a shoulder of dirt, but it all looks like pavement from my perspective. I aim for the middle of the clearing, a bit blinded by the sun, hoping there are no potholes or rocks.

"Does it look like dirt off to the sides?" I ask.

I'm beginning to think it's all solid runway right up to the trees, but that makes no sense.

"It all looks paved to me," replies Margy.

Now I am close enough to see that there are no dirt shoulders. The glare has eased and I can see that the entire clearing is paved in a width that makes Vancouver International look narrow. The runway seems nearly as wide as it is long.

We touch down smoothly. I'm not surprised – my best landings occur when I'm totally focused, paying close attention to runway details.

We taxi off at the only turnout, near mid-field, and pull into the empty parking ramp. A blue pickup truck sits beside the white house trailer near the edge of the ramp.

"There's someone here," states Margy.

"You mean because of the truck, or did you see someone?"

"I saw a man near the trailer. He's gone now."

Great – we find the perfect secluded spot for camping, and the only sign of life within kilometres is right next to us.

We pause in the parking area, engine running at idle.

"What do you think?" I ask.

Margy and I think a lot alike when it comes to camping spots. We don't go camping to socialize, and this guy may not have seen a lot of people lately. The twang of banjos from "Deliverance" drifts through my mind. I have a very active imagination.

"Let's go," she says, probably less concerned for our safety than realizing this place isn't for us.

Without needing further clarification, I know exactly what she means. The only airport within range before dark, the other Bella Bella, is only five kilometres away. So off we go, taxiing back for takeoff. At the end of the runway, I swing the Arrow around, without need for another complete pre-takeoff checklist. While, taxiing, I've reset the pitch and rudder trim and double-checked that my door and the side window are latched. There's little else that needs attention. I advance the throttle, and we rumble back down the runway.

As we climb out over the water, I retract the landing gear (briefly), maneuver back to the Campbell Island airport, and almost immediately turn downwind (gear down almost as soon as it's raised).

Left base leg is over the school's athletic field, and rollout to final points the Arrow's nose straight towards the microwave tower. One way out (downhill) and back in the other way (uphill). We land, back-taxi, and are parked again almost exactly twenty minutes after starting our engine – a round trip cross-country flight of record short duration.

* * * * *

After setting up our tent next to the airplane, our evening stroll is supposed to take us to a small lake off the end of the runway. From there, we should be able to hike down along a creek, which we've identified on the airport diagram, to the floatplane base. But when we get to the end of the runway, it's apparent there is no easy way down from here. The brush in all directions is dense and swampy. As I backtrack up the few metres that I have descended from the runway, I find bear prints and what looks like deer (or elk) tracks. At least it's not a cougar.

That evening, we learn what the locals do at night. They cruise back and forth over the main road, which begins at the ferry terminal and ends at the airport. Every few minutes, we see the lights of their cars turning around at the airport fence; an endless procession of vehicles during the late summer twilight. It's something to do.

Meanwhile, we've found something to do too. We are camped near an old Cessna 320 with a feathered propeller, indicating an in-flight engine failure. Margy examines the airplane closer and reports a series of mysteries that are undoubtedly related – access panels have been removed from the engine that has the feathered prop, and the entire surface of the airframe is unusually deteriorated. The aircraft is old, but not so old that it should be in this condition. I estimate its vintage as mid-1960s. Original aircraft paint holds up better than this in almost any climate, and most aircraft of this model are still flying.

We walk around the aircraft together, noting the condition of the wings and fuselage. The most obvious features (besides the feathered prop) are three flat tires. This plane has sat unattended for years. Through the side window, the instruments can be seen, mostly still in-place. But the center-mounted stack of radios is missing. The rear seats have been removed. Most mysterious of all are the wingtip fuel tanks. Small sawed slices in the fiberglass are evident at the ends of both tanks.

We sit by our tent, putting together possible scenarios. There was an in-flight engine failure, and the pilot landed here successfully. Mechanics tried to fix the failed engine through the missing access panels. Or the aircraft crashed nearby. If so, why is the landing gear fully intact, as well as the underbelly antennas? Or maybe the aircraft ditched into the ocean and was hauled out here. The pilot may have elected to contact the water surface with his landing gear retracted (a wise decision), explaining the lack of landing gear damage but not explaining the intact underbelly antennas. If the airplane was submerged in salt water, that might explain the deteriorated exterior. But nothing explains why the airplane is still here.

The plane carries a U.S. N-number, leading us to speculate on suspicious activity. Drug running from the States might explain an abandoned twin-engine aircraft.

In the morning, we take on a full load of gas, and the fuel attendant has some of the answers we are seeking. In the process, he raises even more questions.

This gas attendant was at the airport five years ago when the twin-engine airplane made an emergency landing. He describes it as a perfect single-engine landing, the feathered propeller standing at attention on the non-rotating engine at touchdown. Feathering is a conscious emergency response made by a pilot, designed to stop the engine from rotating, thus preventing further damage while (more importantly) reducing drag from the otherwise useless windmilling prop.

The pilot exited the aircraft with a severe limp. (I missed the point here, but it seemed to be a suspicious clue in the eyes of the fuel attendant.) Accompanying the pilot were his wife and two children.

The pilot stated they were on a non-stop flight from Alaska to Seattle (in itself, unusual for an aircraft of this limited range). That afternoon, the pilot placed his wife and one child on the next Pacific Coastal flight out. He stayed in town and departed with the second child the next morning. That afternoon, two men arrived in a private airplane, removed a lot of equipment from the twin-Cessna, and departed within a few hours.

The following morning, two RCMP officers appeared on the scene. The aircraft owner (not the pilot) was an Alaskan resident, currently in prison for drug smuggling. The officers proceeded to inspect the aircraft for drugs, including (I assume) cutting open the wingtip fuel tanks, a possible storage location for contraband. They found nothing. In classic frontier style, the case was closed.

The airplane sat unclaimed for several years and finally went up for auction. One buyer bid $35,000 but never showed up. A second prospective purchaser from California arrived in Bella Bella to see what he'd be getting for his $25,000 bid. After seeing the airplane, he changed his offer to $10,000, but it was rejected. As he laughingly noted: "I just spent $2000 on a trip to a one-horse town to see a worthless airplane."

The twin-Cessna sits and deteriorates further in the gravel at Bella Bella Airport, seemingly forgotten by all. If you decide to buy it, bring lots of tools and an abundance of time.

◊ ◊ ◊ ◊ ◊ ◊ ◊

Chapter 2

George on the Raincoast

Airplanes, like people, become acclimated to their surroundings. An Air Force exercise many years ago proves this point. My California Air National Guard unit deployed four C-130s to Alaska in January. The Wyoming Air National Guard sent four more C-130s to join us for an airlift mission that lasted two weeks. It was one of the most frustrating airlift exercises of my military career.

Since I was the officer responsible for the maintenance of the California aircraft, I endured problems related to equipment acclimatization. Not only did our warm-blooded California mechanics suffer in the cold, our airplanes were an embarrassment, requiring a lot of extra work to maintain.

On a typical morning, we'd begin preheating the propellers well before dawn with ground combustion heaters, pumping hot air through a maze of huge ducts up into the hubs of the hydraulic props. More heater-hose snaked, like umbilical cords, into the cockpit and below the flight deck, warming the black boxes that drive the avionics.

It was all to no avail. Our props puked up their hydraulic fluid, and instrument gyros refused to spin. Meanwhile, the pilots from Wyoming, wearing unzipped flight jackets and kick-ass (but unauthorized) cowboy boots, strode out to their airplanes. Like trusty steeds, their airplanes were always ready to fly, with no heaters anywhere. They'd crank their engines and depart on schedule, while we struggled to get our C-130s airborne. The cowboys and their aircraft were the stars of the mission, hands down. And I was left answering to the General for the poor performance of our California C-130s. It's enough to make you believe that equipment that operates fine in warm environments may refuse to cooperate at all in cold conditions.

Now I'm reliving that nightmare with my Piper Arrow. Her first winter in Canada is extended by wave after wave of autumn storms marching down the coast from the Gulf of Alaska. A mid-November flight from Powell River to California seems realistic, if I can find a wide enough weather window. But day-after-day, the storms roll through, never clearing in between. My well-equipped Arrow and 6000 hours of flying experience are adequate for flight inside clouds, but not ones laced with heavy ice and turbulence. In the end, time runs out, and Pacific Coastal and Alaska Airlines shuttle me south.

On the morning Margy and I depart on Pacific Coastal, savage weather is encountered during our climb out of Powell River. It's a wise decision to be inside this stocky turboprop equipped with anti-ice equipment rather than a Piper Arrow. The ride to Vancouver is nerve-wracking, with my hands clenched on the armrests the entire way. After you've flown your own airplane, it's hard to relax in the cabin of an airliner during turbulence. I'm used to taking charge of the Arrow and being in control of the situation. Now my mind is flying the route, but there's nothing for my hands to do except grab the sides of my seat.

The Arrow's first winter in British Columbia is aggravated by the hangar accommodations. Our accumulation of stuff exceeds the footprint of the assigned space. An old 22-foot boat, *Gemini*, sits on blocks in the hangar, awaiting refurbishment. An empty boat trailer and a utility trailer sporting two quads fill up most of the remaining space. Mr. Float Cabin, a bookmobile that John is building for me, will need to be sandwiched in somewhere. In addition, when we are in the States, the hangar is also the storage location for Margy's truck. There's hardly room to breath, say nothing of finding room for an airplane. So the Arrow is evicted from her proper home.

Since July, our airplane has been tied down outside, next to the Westview Flying Club's Cessna 172. The club's aircraft, known as "ETL," will weather the winter outside with our Arrow. (It's hard to imagine how Canadian pilots and air traffic controllers handle this constant barrage of letters. ETL's full radio call sign is "Charlie Golf Echo Tango Lima" (C-GETL), a real mouthful compared to typical U.S. numeric call signs.)

The outside spot is nice for the Arrow during the summer, since she can sit and watch all of the airport action. But now winter is coming on fast, with no hope of getting the airplane back to California. I remind myself that our Arrow has sat outside during winters in California, so this is nothing new. Then again, this is the Raincoast.

I'm particularly concerned about moisture in the cabin. Pipers have a tendency to leak, particularly through the entry door and all of the side window seals. There is also a mysterious accumulation of water that tends to seep through the wing root and into the baggage area. For years I've fought these problems, but never solved them. In California, leakage was controlled by the use of an exterior cabin cover. But this isn't California.

In the Bayliner, I've minimized the problem of winter moisture with desiccant crystals. But boats are meant to get wet. Aircraft avionics, on the other hand, are quickly degraded when exposed to moisture.

Using desiccant seems a reasonable solution, so I purchase the crystals and a plastic container at my local pilot shop (Canadian Tire). As the winter proceeds, regular accumulation of water in the collection dish indicates that it's working. What I don't realize is that the moisture is also collecting elsewhere, especially under the cockpit glare-shield where many of the critical avionics components are mounted.

In December, after returning to Powell River, I find the airplane's desiccant container relatively dry, but the carpet is soaked. The aircraft logbooks, stored on the floor behind the copilot's seat, are water-damaged and mildewed. I visualize other areas invaded by moisture, including the instrument panel and the navigation boxes mounted in the tailcone behind the baggage compartment.

At the December meeting of the Westview Flying Club, Tyrone makes a presentation regarding ETL. He's in charge of the club's airplane and is concerned that the aircraft is sitting outside this winter, a victim of the hangar wait-list. In the interest of financial survival, the club has leased hangar space to recreational vehicle owners. Now the club's own Cessna is homeless. But Canadian airplanes are used to living outside, and the club's officers are more concerned about the eviction of paying customers. They agree to find hangar-space for ETL as soon as possible, but that won't be right away.

In the meantime, Tyrone (who treats the aircraft like his own) reports he has installed a 60-watt light bulb to keep interior moisture to a minimum. He notes that this simple improvement has already paid dividends. A radio with problematic reception now seems to be working again.

I listen to this discussion and visualize the Arrow collecting moisture in her critical areas. It's time to get serious about the problem. After the meeting, I talk to some of the club's members about how to handle interior moisture in this environment.

"You just have to live with it," says Dale. "Ventilate the cabin the best you can when the sun shines, and get your bird airborne as often as possible. The more an airplane sits, the worse it gets."

That's good advice, but winter storms keep moving through without a break. I resolve to fly the Arrow as soon as possible.

"I had a radio problem similar to ETL's," says Selina. "I took the radio home and warmed it in the oven for a while, and it worked fine after that."

So in Canada, you solve radio problems by cooking them. Heat is the obvious solution, and warmth from a single light bulb can do a lot.

"Just hook up to ETL's electrical cord," offers Tyrone.

What I like about our flying club is how quickly we solve problems. It doesn't take a board of directors meeting to get things moving.

The next day I mount a shop light with a 60-watt bulb inside the Arrow. Clipped onto one of the seat belts, it shines warm rays towards the avionics panel. To conserve electricity, I install a timer to activate the bulb only during the night.

I return a few days later, after another rainstorm. When I open the cabin door, warm air pours out. The carpet is no longer soaked, and the dry air is undoubtedly permeating the whole interior, including the critical avionics area behind the baggage compartment. I hope it isn't too late.

* * * * *

The winter rains are relentless. There is hardly a break before I return to California for Christmas. There are occasional flyable days, but they usually find me at my float cabin on Powell Lake. The Arrow will need to sit through another trip to the States, although now the 60-watt bulb is keeping the interior relatively dry.

I return to California, again by airline, and our Arrow stays behind, resting in her outside tie-down on the Raincoast. When I return to Powell River in early February, there is finally a sunny day, although a cold one.

Margy and I untie the Arrow and pull her forward from the soaked grass onto the pavement. I'm not even sure the battery has survived the prolonged cold with enough charge to start the engine.

As Margy goes through the pre-start checklist, I reach overhead for my shoulder harness. The strap is jammed in its inertial retraction reel. I give it a sharp tug, but it is locked in place. While I pull on the strap, I notice Margy has stopped reading the checklist. She too is pulling on her shoulder harness to no avail. Both of our inertial reels are locked in the retracted position. She gives me an inquisitive look.

"Frozen, I guess," I say, in response to her gaze. "The grease in the reels must be congealed from the cold."

It has been particularly cold lately, but today it is sunny, and the cockpit feels almost spring-like warm. We haven't even tried to start the engine, and already we are grounded.

"How do you feel about flying without a shoulder harness?" I ask.

There are regulations, and there is reality. This airplane has independent seat belts and shoulder harnesses, and the belts are fine. Some older airplanes don't even have shoulder harnesses. But if you have them, you're supposed to use them, at least for takeoff and landing. That's the rule in the States. I'm not even sure it's a requirement in Canada, but certainly it's uncomfortable (to me) to fly without a shoulder harness.

"I'm okay with it, if you are," replies Margy.

It's just a flight in the local area under near-perfect weather conditions. It's more like driving 55 kilometres per hour in a 50-klick zone than blasting through an intersection on yellow. I'm reluctant to bend any rule of flight, to say nothing of breaking one, but it would be a shame not to take advantage of this fair weather anomaly and give this airplane a much-needed dry-out flight. Once we're airborne, the airflow through the cabin will do wonders. There may not be another opportunity for weeks, maybe months.

"Let's continue with the checklist," I say. "We'll stay local and go without the harnesses."

The Arrow's engine cranks amazingly well, starting on the first rotation of the prop. The motor's initial warm-up is rough, but within seconds it is firing on all four cylinders.

As usual, I let Margy run the checklist and prepare for the takeoff. This gives me a chance to monitor the engine gauges and set up the avionics. Most novices find landings to be the adrenaline-producing moments of flight. For me, it is the takeoff that is most critical. Maximum engine power is essential during this segment of flight, so I watch the cylinder head temperatures (CHT) and all engine gauges closely. Having another pilot to fly the airplane during takeoff is a wonderful luxury.

While the engine goes through its initial warm-up, I flip on the alternator switch and then the avionics master. I'm greeted by flashing lights on the flight director annunciator panel. Now there's something I've never seen before.

The Arrow's flight director is distinctive. Few single-engine aircraft have such a system, an avionics suite usually reserved for airliners. But N41997 boasts a fully functional flight director for advanced navigation and autopilot control. It's a bit of overkill for a Piper Arrow, but an extravagance you quickly learn to enjoy. In fact, after using a flight director, it's nearly impossible to taxi to the runway without it.

When I first met Daniel, a young Pacific Coastal pilot, I couldn't wait to show him my Arrow's flight director. Daniel grew up around airplanes of all types, and he knows it's unusual to find command bars and mode annunciators in a small airplane. So one night, after his last airline flight of the day, we stumble around the Arrow with a crappy flashlight that requires an occasional slap against my thigh to keep the beam shining.

"What do you think?" I ask as I open the airplane's door, shining the light inside.

So far, I haven't told him what to expect, except that my cockpit is "unique."

"Wow!" he says. "Chicken legs."

"Chicken legs?"

"Yeah, the command bars," Daniel replies.

He's right. Yellow command bars pop down on the sides of the FCI (flight command indicator), which is equivalent to a less-sophisti-cated attitude indicator in most small airplanes. They do look like the skinny legs of a chicken. I can never turn on the flight director again without thinking of Daniel's "chicken legs."

Now, on this chilly February day, two of the flight director's mode annunciator lights are burning steady and the BC (back course) and GS (glide slope) lights are flashing. The impossible part of the situation is that the flight director isn't even turned on.

Margy scrunches her face in an skeptical pose.

"Got me," I say, shaking my head in wonder. "Must be moisture in the system."

"Did you turn the flight director on?" Margy asks.

"No, George has a mind of his own today. Either that, or he's lost his mind."

George, the autopilot (and flight director), is our best friend in flight. He's normally very reliable and has bailed us out of situations we should not have entered in the first place.

"I'll pull the circuit breaker," I say, reaching in front of me to deac-tivate George. This is an alternate way to turn George off. Of course, I haven't even turned him on, so electrons must be running along some very unusual paths.

Raincoast winter moisture has taken its toll. Things are quickly going from bad to worse, but there is no safety concern regarding flying without George. But it does make me wonder what else the moisture may have affected.

When I pull the circuit breaker, the annunciator lights go out. Good thing – otherwise, we're infested with goblins.

I suggest we move forward to the far end of the Flying Club's ramp to complete our engine run-up and magneto check, where we will avoid blasting the cars behind us on the other side of the fence. Margy releases the brakes and rolls forward to reposition the airplane.

While Margy finishes the pre-takeoff checklist, I continue to monitor the engine gauges. All is well, so I flip some of the radio switches to the "on" position, hoping for the best. Number 2 communication radio immediately produces annoying background static that should automatically be squelched, but it isn't. So I turn it off. I realize that moisture has soaked into every nook and cranny of the airplane.

Margy hasn't even progressed to the magneto check when she stops.

"The trim is frozen," she notes.

I watch as she pushes her thumb on the split trim switch, moving both segments simultaneously. Normally, the stabilator trim wheel between our seats would move as a result, but the wheel sits idle.

"Try it manually," I suggest.

She reaches down to the trim wheel and tries to rotate it with her hand.

"Won't move," she says.

I reach between the seats and try to move the wheel. It is not merely tight – the wheel is frozen in position. At some point, minor problems spell out an obvious message. Today's message is clear: Don't fly!

Two jammed inertial reels are barely acceptable for a local flight. George is unnecessary for such a flight, and we have another communication radio. But a frozen trim is more serious. Besides, what else lurks in the wiring?

"Let's taxi to the shop," I state with finality.

Our dry-out flight has been short. In fact, our entire route consists of a taxi path from the Flying Club ramp to the Suncoast Aviation maintenance shop.

* * * * *

The next day, the chief mechanic provides the verdict.

"That California thick grease won't hack it here," says Kevin. "It traps moisture and clumps up like tar. The stabilator trim jackscrew was caked with frozen grease, so we scooped it out like putty. Then we used thinner lubricant, and it works fine now."

Similarly, the inertial reels are repaired by disassembly and lubrication. But George is another subject altogether.

"Avionics are prone to all kinds of moisture problems in our wet winters," notes Kevin. "Usually, all it takes is just a bit of time to let them dry out, but I'm not so sure about your flight director."

The system is intricate and dependent upon the perfect integration of multiple electronic components. George's brain is temporarily bewildered by erroneous inputs from his nervous system, a wiring scheme nearly as complicated as a human's. Unless he fixes himself (about as likely as a nervous-breakdown fixing itself), he will need major repairs. George has no Canadian social insurance card, so I don't look forward to quick and inexpensive surgery.

* * * * *

We finally get airborne at the next major break in the weather in early March. The trim works fine, and we have operable shoulder harnesses.

We leave the local traffic pattern and fly across the Strait of Georgia to Courtney Airpark. During the short flight, I open all of the vents and turn the heater and defroster on full-blast. The warm, dry airflow will do wonders for the airplane, but it is too-little too-late for George. I push the autopilot circuit breaker in, and the annunciator panel lights repeat their strange blinking sequence. Maybe all will be better after this dry-out flight, but for now I pull the circuit breaker again.

Courtney sits beneath the heavy military traffic pattern of the nearby Canadian Forces Base at Comox. We slip into the small airport's downwind leg just as a four-engine P-3 drones down the Comox approach path, nearly overhead. Below us, Courtney beckons – a quaint little airport with a runway barely long enough for a fully-loaded Piper Arrow

On the ground, we hike the path around the airport's perimeter, observing the numerous species of birds that frequent this peninsula. Floatplanes takeoff and land on the adjacent slough that leads upstream

to a small harbour and downtown Courtney. It's a place to spend hours of relaxation, watching boats, birds, and airplanes. Add to the menu a personable airport cafe, and you have a very satisfying day.

When it's time to depart, I ask Margy to let me do the takeoff, and she readily agrees. It isn't an airstrip she can't handle, particularly since we are well under gross weight today. But we'll still take up nearly the entire runway on takeoff. The departure route to the south is flat and thankfully over water, so I get airborne as quickly as possible, and level off in the slightly compressed air between the wing and the pavement. I accelerate in "ground effect" until most of the runway is behind us. Then I begin the climb out over the water.

Now we're back under the Comox arrival path and then upward and across the strait towards Texada's Blubber Bay and then Powell River. On the flight home, I reset the flight director's circuit breaker once again. Blinking annunciator lights greet me.

With all of George's switches still off, his brain is still mysteriously active. The command bars (chicken legs!) are helplessly tilted below the horizon, and none of the buttons are functional.

When it's time to depart for California again, it will be a long flight back without George's assistance. It's enough to make a pilot humble.

◊ ◊ ◊ ◊ ◊ ◊

Chapter 3

Alpha Route to Victoria

"November four-one-niner-niner-seven is cleared to the Victoria Airport, Alpha one-six, Nanaimo, Alpha one, Victoria. Climb and maintain seven thousand, squawk five-six-six-seven. Departure frequency will be one-two-three decimal seven."

I read back the clearance to Comox Terminal on my cell phone, with the engine running, sitting in the run-up area adjacent to the Westview Flying Club. Margy continues the pre-departure checklist, while I receive the remaining instructions from Comox.

"How soon can you be airborne?" asks the voice on the phone.

"Five minutes, maximum," I reply.

Margy has finished the engine run-up and is working on the last few items on the checklist.

"That'll work fine. You're released now, with clearance void if not off by one-seven-five-zero Zulu. Time now is one-seven-four-one."

I read back the essentials: "Released now. Clearance void at one-seven-five-zero. Thanks for the clearance. See you on frequency in a few minutes."

"We'll talk to you airborne. Have a good flight."

It's a beautiful, clear June morning, but I prefer instrument flight rules wherever I go. It's challenging, keeps me current on procedures, and is actually a lot easier in a high density traffic environment. Victoria isn't Vancouver, but it can get busy, and the radar controllers will lead me right up to final alignment with the runway. Besides, filing IFR on the Internet is getting easier, now that I've gotten used to the Canadian version of flight plans and have stored a few routes that are easily modified. A quick point-and-click with the flight plan software, and we're on our way.

I go back on headset, and talk to Margy.

"Clearance is the standard departure route," I say. "We've got almost ten minutes before our clearance void time. Are you ready to taxi?"

"Takeoff checklist is complete. Which way?"

We both know which runway we'll use, since the windsock clearly favors a takeoff to the west. To taxi for departure at Powell River, you must use the active runway because there is no parallel taxiway. But there is a choice on how to get there. If the route to the terminal is unobstructed, it's best to taxi past Oceanview Helicopters to stay off the runway as long as possible. Today no rotors stick out from the normally busy pads near the Flying Club.

"Let's taxi past the terminal," I reply. "If you'll do the takeoff, I'll take care of the radios."

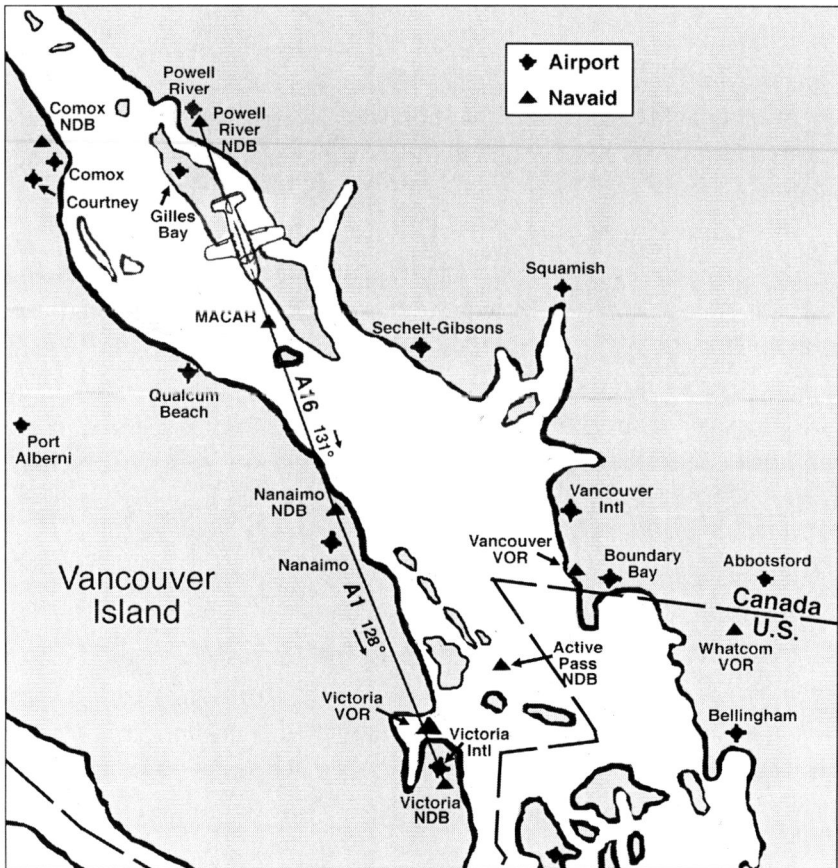

This is the norm for us. I'd rather talk, navigate, and monitor the engine gauges than fly. Besides, Margy makes excellent takeoffs, so our system works well.

"Anything special regarding the fuel pump?" asks Margy as she begins taxiing towards the terminal.

A few minutes ago, engine start was far from normal. The clicking sound of the electric fuel pump was missing when Margy flipped the switch before engine start, and there was no indication of fuel pressure. At that point, we found the pump's circuit breaker popped, but resetting it didn't solve the problem. It took some unusual maneuvering of the throttle and mixture levers to get the engine running.

"No, just leave the pump off, and I'll monitor fuel pressure closely during the takeoff and climb. Technically, we should abort, but we've got some experience with this."

"I remember – all the way back from Baja," she replies. "I know it's safe."

"We'll take the airplane to the shop when we get back from Victoria. But for now, we've got a good engine-driven pump, with no electrical backup."

There's no gravity-feed with the Piper's wing tanks mounted below the engine, but suction pressure provides a positive flow. So in addition to our functioning engine-driven pump, we have a natural backup. It wouldn't be a good day for loops and chandelles, but I feel comfortable with the situation.

If Margy concurs with our departure under these circumstances, it will make me feel more at ease. In our challenge-and-response system in the cockpit, my attitude of sometimes overlooking the details is nicely tempered by her let's-look-at-this-closer point of view.

"So you're okay with it?" I ask.

"I'm fine," replies Margy.

If she weren't, she would be quick to speak up. We're a good team that way – using a two-for-two vote to verify any decision related to safety. It's bailed us out of a few potentially bad decisions. I'm pleased with our consensus regarding the electric fuel pump. Knowing airplanes, it might even start working again, just as mysteriously as it stopped.

Margy taxis to the approach end of Runway 27, does a U-turn, flips on the transponder, sets the brakes, and then applies full power.

"Doors?" she asks, before releasing the brakes.

"Locked," I reply, as I verify the latch setting on my door by reaching up and touching the handle. As we accelerate, I monitor the engine gauges, noting that the fuel pressure is right where it should be.

We're airborne by midfield. Margy is already retracting the landing gear when I see John in front of our hangar. He's working on our boat today (*Gemini*), and gives us a full arm wave, which I return with as much hand movement as possible in the small cockpit. I know his eagle eyes see me wave back.

This flight is an excuse to get in the air. We haven't flown in three weeks, it's a gorgeous day, and there's book business for me in Victoria.

Margy makes the left turn for a crosswind departure, our path now parallel between Joyce Avenue and the shoreline.

"Give Helen and Ed a wing-wag, and not a wimpy one," I joke.

Margy uses both hands to make a firm waggle of our wings, two complete wing-rocking cycles. It's definitely not wimpy.

Then it's upward over Texada Island, as I contact the air traffic control facility at Comox. We join A16, the non-directional beacon route to Nanaimo. Alpha routes (also called amber routes because of their color on charts) are unique to Canada. In the States you'll never fly such a route based on NDB station locations. It's an older style of navigation, but it works well for Canada, especially when backed up these days by GPS.

Over the Nanaimo NDB, we make a small heading correction, and I reset the GPS to A1, an amber route that leads to Victoria Ladysmith Harbour spreads out below us to the right, and Dodd Narrows is straight ahead. Water is running strong through the passage, flooding northward and producing its typical whitecaps in the narrow channel. What can't be seen are the swirling currents and whirlpools, but I know they are present. Two boats are entering Dodd Narrows, in line from the south, pushing forward on a flooding tide. It's easy to handle, if you know what you're doing. But the swift current is not for amateurs.

We pass over the Gulf Islands, with fair-weather cumulus dotting the skyline in puffy patches. Near Duncan, I watch a cute little tugboat without a barge plowing through the shoreline waters, generating a substantial wake in the nearly calm sea.

Victoria Terminal is busy providing radar vectors to an Air Canada jet headed for Vancouver International and several smaller aircraft just passing through, but they efficiently work us into the flow of traffic. We are assigned a heading that takes us towards Victoria for a wide left base leg to align with the Runway 09 visual approach. It's a quick way into the airport.

"Niner-niner-seven is cleared for the visual approach to Runway Zero-Niner, not below three thousand until established on final."

I read back the clearance, and Margy intercepts the final approach course and begins the descent. We're handed off to the control tower. On short final, we pass over the floatplane base at Mill Bay.

Then we're on the ground and taxiing to the Aero Centre near the Victoria Flying Club. When ground control gives us our final turn and we are within sight of the ramp, I call the Aero Centre Unicom. A parking assistant is already there, waiting to marshal us into a spot near a Citation Bravo jet.

I've called ahead for a car rental for the 20-kilometre trip to downtown. It's really Sidney's airport rather than Victoria's, making it a bit of a drive to town.

Inside the Aero Centre, the woman at the counter kids me about my red *Canada* cap: "This car will match your hat. It's a red Mustang."

"Do they send my speeding tickets to you or me?" I jest. "You don't think I look like a tourist in this hat, do you?"

It's hard to hide your nationality when you're traveling through Canada in an airplane with an N-number, clearly indicating U.S. registration.

We load our backpacks into the Mustang, and then walk over to one of my favorite spots, the Victoria Flying Club,. Their small bookstore has interesting aviation books, clothing, and charts. I buy a copy of the latest version of Transport Canada's *Aeronautical Information Manual* and a hat with *YVR* (Vancouver Airport) above the brim to replace my Canada tourist hat. It's still a tourist hat, but at least designed for aviation tourists.

"Wish we had YYJ hats," says the sales clerk, referring to the designator for Victoria.

"I don't see any BC airport guide books here," I reply.

"No, we don't have any. I don't think there is such a book, but there should be. Somebody should write one."

"I am," I reply.

She looks at me with a bit of suspicion, and I doubt she believes me. I wonder whether she's reading this now?

* * * * *

Leaving the airport, we pass Mary's Bleue Moon Cafe across from the air museum. It's one of my favorite restaurants. The parking lot is busy now, during lunch-hour, but it should be easy to get seats for an early dinner. It'll be worth a try during our trip back to the airport.

On the way to Victoria, we pass Elk Lake. The small recreational lake reminds me of Puddingstone Reservoir in California, and it causes me to reflect on the differences between big cities and Powell River. Puddingstone is located adjacent to our home airport in California. After takeoff, noise abatement procedures require an immediate left turn of 20 degrees to over-fly the Puddingstone Dam and to avoid the campground.

I wonder if Elk Lake, like Puddingstone, has an urban getaway atmosphere. Puddingstone is a recreational oasis in the heart of the Los Angeles sprawl, allowing boats on odd-numbered days, with even-days reserved for jet skis. I doubt Victoria's Elk Lake is as crowded as Puddingstone, but it's a far cry from the remote Elk Lake near Powell River. A hand-made wooden sign points to that Elk Lake, and it takes a major effort to navigate the trail to get there.

I haven't been far from Powell River for over a month, so I'm awed by the bustle of traffic. One freeway sign reads: *Quadra Street – 1000 metres*. It's a huge sign. Wouldn't *1 Km* make more sense and reduce the size of the sign? I love to be critical of those who inhabit big cities, a criticism I consider allowable, considering my city-folk background.

In downtown Victoria, I meet with Shannon, a representative of Printorium BookWorks, regarding the upcoming print-run of my next book. In the process, I encounter another example of how closely entwined people are in coastal BC.

It always amazes me to be constantly running into people I know in Powell River. Such occasions seldom occur in Los Angeles, and it is, of course, part of living in a small town environment. Today I learn that Shannon was born and raised in Powell River (a moderate coincidence) and that her mother is Carla Mobley, author of *Mysterious Powell Lake* (a major coincidence). Carla's book is a historic account (now out of print) of characters on the lake. As the author of *Up the Lake*, I'm amazed by the Powell River connection, right here in downtown Victoria.

I ask Shannon for directions to Trafford Publications. I have no business to discuss with the publisher today, but I'd like to visit the vine-covered building I've seen on Trafford's web site. The building is less than a kilometre from Printorium, and Shannon notes that I'll want to go inside to see if Tyee, the dog, is in the building. Tyee is famous on Trafford logos, and I visualize a photo of Tyee and me for my personal files.

At the corner of Bay and Government, I locate the Trafford building. Yes, it is ivy-covered. No, it doesn't look like a publishing office. But inside, it's obvious that these are book-friendly people.

"I'm one of your authors," I remark as I introduce myself to the receptionist.

I can tell she is impressed.

"I'm in Victoria on other business today, and I want to get a photo of Tyee, if he's here."

Now here's a subject she can understand. The dog is quite a celebrity around here.

"Oh, Tyee isn't here today," she says.

A giant painting of Tyee spreads across the wall in the reception area, so I'll have to settle for second-best. I ask Margy to take a picture of me in front of the mural. If I can't have the real thing, at least his portrait is impressive.

* * * * *

On the way back to the airport, we stop at a WalMart, reinforcing the big city aspect of today's visit to Victoria. Powell River has a WalMart, but this store is huge by comparison. I walk the aisles, marveling at the variety of products. In some ways, I feel like an alien space traveler visiting another planet, encountering unexpected technology and outrageous extravagance.

We arrive back at the airport at 5 pm, and Mary's Bleue Moon Cafe is not crowded, so we pick a seat near an unbelievably clean wall-mounted radial engine. It's a nine-cylinder powerful beast, with polished brass pushrods. The engine was previously installed on a DeHavilland Beaver. How can an engine so brutish look so beautiful? It's hangs on the wall as a gorgeous piece of art.

A sign near the entry boasts the specials of the day, including: *Hi Balls $2.95*. This unique cafe was established in 1939, when airplanes landed in the field across the street and the pilots walked to Mary's Coffee Bar. It's still a popular spot. The Alberta beef ribs and berry pie are my favorites, making Victoria Airport worth a stop just for these delicacies alone.

Back at the Aero Centre, I turn in the rental car keys and pay our aircraft gas bill. The Arrow is sitting outside the large glass doors, with a Pikachu pillow (emblazoned with the friendly little monster) sticking upright in the side window. Leave it to those silly Americans.

We load the back of the aircraft with our WalMart purchases, which includes two poster frames, fenders for our boat, and a large glass bottle with a watermelon painted on it – necessities all. Margy does the preflight, while I organize the cargo.

The electric fuel pump is working now. Not only is it operational, even the sound of the pump is normal, a good indicator of it's condition. Almost always, the pump will make unusual noises before it fails. This evening, it is clicking along with a healthy, steady beat. I turn the pump on and off several times, and it no longer pops the circuit breaker. It's a good start for the flight home, but it goes downhill from there.

"I can't find anything on file for you," states the clearance delivery controller, as we sit in the Aero Centre ramp with our engine running. "What was your proposed departure time, and how did you file?"

"I filed for zero-one-thirty Zulu, and I used the Internet equivalent of U.S. DUATS." It's a fumbling reply, but he knows I'm a U.S. pilot by my N-number. Canadian Internet filing is probably not called DUATS.

"Well, I don't have anything on you, so you'll have to shut down and go back inside to file IFR or telephone Vancouver Terminal for a VFR transponder code."

I'm stuck, and the engine is running. We've come this far in the departure process (the hardest part), and now we have to start all over again. I'm not looking forward to the delay, which will likely be extensive. Maybe there's an alternative.

"Is it possible for me to coordinate here on the ramp by cell phone?" I ask. "I can file a VFR flight note with a friend in Powell River and notify you when that's complete."

"Roger, Nine-nine-seven, but you'll still need the transponder code from Vancouver Terminal. They have to provide that code to you on the telephone."

I see where he is headed with this discussion, but there may still be hope.

"Yes, I understand. But could you give me Vancouver Terminal's telephone number, and I'll complete both calls while taxiing for departure."

Those hurry-up Americans! Then I think of something that may make this controller feel better about my proposal: "We have two pilots aboard, so one can taxi while the other makes the phone calls."

Pause. More pause.

"Okay, nine-nine-seven. Yes, that would be okay with us. Taxi to Runway Zero-Niner. Hold short of Runway Two-Zero, and let me know when you are ready to copy the Vancouver Terminal phone number."

Success! I haven't had a lot of luck with Canadian flight plan procedures in recent months, but maybe I now know enough to be innovative. Certainly this sounds like something that not many Canadian pilots do on a regular basis.

I'm on the cell phone now, headset off, explaining to Vancouver Terminal that we are taxiing at Victoria Airport and looking for a departure code. Again, my N-number is a tip-off that I'm an American, so I feel it's necessary to explain.

"I thought I had an instrument clearance waiting for me, but it has fallen out of the system. So I'm trying to avoid shutting down, if I can proceed VFR with a code from you."

As I speak, it really doesn't make a lot of sense to me, so I don't expect him to understand.

"So you're looking for a new instrument clearance?" he asks.

"No, no. A VFR code would be perfect."

I get my code, with a few momentary delays while Vancouver verifies my aircraft type and cruising altitude to Powell River. I notice Margy has momentarily stopped where the parallel taxiway crosses Runway 20, but now she is proceeding again, following a Boeing 737 to Runway 9.

When I hang up, I give Margy a thumbs-up (still can't talk to her without my headset), and she nods. Then I place the phone call to John.

"Hey, John!" I say when he answers. "I'm taxiing towards the runway at Victoria, and I need to file a flight notice with a responsible party."

"That's me," he replies.

He doesn't even question why I'm talking to him while taxiing in an airplane. But he's familiar with the flight notification process that I've used with him on many VFR flights. It requires a telephone closeout with John after my arrival. If we don't get there when expected, John won't hesitate to launch search and rescue.

"I'll give you a wing-wag on the way in at about 7:30, but I'll also call or come by your house after I land."

"Okay, man."

"And don't forget the procedures. If we don't show up, call somebody. Maybe the FBI."

He'd like that. John laughs, says something about "Nice and clear here" that is difficult to understand over the noise of the engine, and then hangs up. I put my headset back on and ask Margy what I've missed on the radio.

"They want us to pull off at the turnout at the end. Something about eagles that need to be cleared from the area before the next 737 departs."

That explains the fire truck headed our way on the taxiway. Between the truck and us is another WestJet 737, now on the parallel taxiway. I call ground control to explain our situation: "I have the squawk code from Vancouver, and I've filed my VFR flight note with a responsible party in Powell River."

"Roger, nine-nine-seven. Hold for WestJet, and I can get you out behind him. Will you be ready for an immediate departure, if I can arrange a left turn as soon as you're airborne, reference the jet?"

I glance at Margy, who nods affirmatively, and then reply.

"We'll be ready behind WestJet."

We'll be ready, but what does an immediate departure mean when following a commercial jet? In the States, there would be a departure delay for the wake turbulence to settle, no matter what. I assume the same rules apply here.

Meanwhile, there is some confusion on the frequency, as a small aircraft reports he is on Runway 20 and requests an immediate takeoff. Maybe he has become confused by the controller's instructions for us. I picture the aircraft sitting in the middle of the runway without a clearance, ready to takeoff.

"Foxtrot-Delta-Hotel, don't move!" says the controller. "I have a 737 departing on Runway Zero Nine."

One thing about Canadian controllers: when things get tight, they use lingo you can understand.

The second 737 stops next to us, and I snap a photo. But before the fire truck arrives, the airliner taxis onto the runway. Somebody has decided the eagles are no longer a problem.

As soon as the 737 begins its takeoff roll, we're cleared onto the runway: "Position and wait," terminology I enjoy in contrast to the U.S. "Position and hold," although the meaning is the same.

We pull into position on Runway 09, as the 737 rotates airborne at the other end of the runway, and the controller doesn't delay an instant longer.

"Nine-nine-seven, cleared for immediate takeoff, with a climbing left turn when airborne."

These guys don't mess around. There's already another aircraft lined up behind us for landing on Runway 09.

Often, in situations like this, Margy defers the takeoff to me. But this evening she feels confident in a slot that's closely-spaced behind a commercial jet and another aircraft on final, with the additional requirement for a quick turn to avoid the jet's wake turbulence.

We're off and upward. Margy swings the Arrow to the left, climbing over the jumble of land and water that make up the Gulf Islands. Bright sunlight floods the cockpit. We're headed home to Powell River, where the pace is a lot slower, and life is a lot simpler.

◊ ◊ ◊ ◊ ◊ ◊ ◊

Chapter 4

Unexpected Destinations

The best destinations in my life have often been found by chance rather than by choice. That is particularly true when traveling by private aircraft. Landing at an unplanned destination due to weather deviations or mechanical problems fits this mold.

Departing Chilko Lake, north of Powell River, leads to such a destination. With only 2500 feet of gravel for a runway and a field elevation of 3850 feet, it's a bit tight on this warm July morning. I have the controls during the takeoff, while Margy handles the checklists and monitors the instruments. Just as the landing gear retracts, there is a loud *pop* accompanied by a reduced rate of climb – not good in this rugged territory.

The airport is still within gliding range, so we continue to climb sluggishly, circling near the runway in an open area over the end of the lake. I initially conclude that the gear has not fully retracted, which would explain the *pop* and the deterioration in the rate of climb. Is the landing gear now jammed in a partially extended position?

This trip is a cross-county formation flight with my friend, David, and another pilot as his passenger, now taking off behind us, so I radio back immediately. David maneuvers up under my aircraft with his airplane (another Arrow) to investigate.

All looks normal to David, but I can't gain altitude at the ordinary rate. We hover together over Chilko Lake, discussing the problem on the air-to-air frequency.

"All looks okay," reports David. "Your gear seems tucked up into the wheel wells."

"Climb performance is poor, only about 100 feet a minute," I answer over the multicom frequency. "But oil pressure and temperature are okay. So let's start out of the valley. You lead, but keep it slow."

The engine sounds smooth, but climb performance is still poor. The landing gear retraction noise may have been just a coincidence, unrelated to the power problem. Maybe it was an engine sound I heard, although it happened just as the gear was retracting.

As we slip out of the valley, over a ridge to the east, David and I talk over the radio, discussing our options. It's nice to have a sunny day, lots of fuel, and a friend flying in formation with you. We head towards the nearest major airport at Kamloops, where a repair facility is located. I follow David through a wide saddle in the mountains that leads us out of the valley.

All is well for the rest of the flight. As we begin our descent into Kamloops, it's time to make our initial radio call to the control tower. Our arrival coincides with the onset of a rain shower. It isn't much of a shower, but big droplets pound hard on the plexiglass windshield. We haven't seen rain (Californians!) in months, so this is a momentous event. I decide to report the shower to the control tower. As usual, we are immediately identified in our communications as Americans by our "N" prefix. In the background, as the controller replies, I hear some chuckling. Those Americans must not see rain very often.

Just before touchdown, as I flare the airplane for landing, I reduce the throttle to idle, and the engine's previous smoothness changes into a fierce vibration. A metre above the pavement is a strange place for this to happen, but a good place.

We taxi to the repair facility and get immediate attention. As a "transient" aircraft, I've always received great maintenance support. I guess it breaks up the day of a bored airplane mechanic to attend to the unscheduled problem of a visitor.

One of the Arrow's cylinders has an exhaust valve stuck open, accounting for the significant drop in power. This has also resulted in a bent push rod. Even with the high priority provided to us by the shop, fixing these problems will require an overnight stay.

We're more interested in camping than staying in a hotel, so we inquire about campgrounds and local sites of interest. We're told about a nearby unique spot, Anglemont Airport. The process of getting there will take some careful planning.

David flies to Anglemont, drops his passenger and all of our combined camping gear, and then returns to Kamloops to pick up Margy and me. He has a grin on his face that he refuses to explain, except to say: "Wait 'til you see this place!"

Final approach to Anglemont is over a lake. It is the only clear approach to the small airport, since the runway begins near the water's edge and runs uphill on a 12-percent slope. That may not sound like much of an incline, but there is an infamous sloped airport in the States (Catalina Island) that's barely more than 5 percent. With 12 percent (which computes out as 11 degrees), it would be possible to land a Boeing 737 and get it stopped in the length of this short runway. But once committed to landing at Anglemont, there are absolutely no go-around options, so your first shot at the runway better be good.

We are soon down and setting up camp at one of the world's most unusual airports. Later that evening, as we sit around the campfire, we marvel at the inclined runway and think about taking off in the morning.

The next day, it will take two shuttle flights to get us back to Kamloops, so we start the day early. Taxiing uphill for a downhill takeoff requires nearly full power. The takeoff is like an elevator ride. We are off the ground within 300 feet of forward travel, assisted by the slingshot effect of gravity. The remaining runway disappears behind us at an amazing angle. I have always wished I could experience a takeoff from an aircraft carrier. This is a close simulation.

The best places you ever visit are often unscheduled destinations. If it hadn't been for an engine malfunction, we never would have found this airport. Since our visit to Anglemont, this great little airfield has been closed, so I'll never be able to go there again. It's a sad loss for British Columbia aviation.

* * * * *

Twin Lakes appears to be a perfect camping location. When looking for overnight stops, a runway within walking distance of a lake is always a good sign. The Canadian *VFR Flight Supplement* is a great source of information about geographic features within the immediate vicinity of airports. The small airfield diagrams include an overview of nearby terrain, including roads, rivers, and lakes. Even on the less-detailed VFR chart, Twin Lakes (east of Chilko Lake, BC) looks ideal. The *Flight Supplement* shows the runway nestled between two small lakes. Each end of the 3600-foot turf strip is near water's edge.

From overhead, after a two-hour flight from Alert Bay, we encounter an unexpected problem. Near mid-field, a building that seemed nondescript in the *Flight Supplement* diagram, has *Twin Lakes* painted on the roof. It looks like a large recreational lodge. Maybe this airport, designated as "Public" in the *Supplement*, is a lot more populated than we had expected. (Twin Lakes Airport is another uniquely located BC airport that has since been closed.)

Margy turns the controls of the airplane over to me for the approach, which is our standard procedure for a destination like this. She does almost all of the takeoffs, but I get many of the landings, especially those that are most challenging. Both of us prefer it that way. Overall, Margy logs more flight hours on trips like this than I do, but I relish handling the tough landings. For the most part, I'm content to take care of flight plans, IFR navigation, and ATC communications, with an occasional highly-demanding approach and landing.

In this case, I get an easier-than-expected challenge on a strip with wide-open approaches at both ends. But the 4000-foot field elevation will make the takeoff the next day marginal, unless we depart before the sun gets very high. Airports like these become takeoff hazards when the hot summer air thins over the airfoils. However, such departures are usually easily handled in the cool of the morning.

The approach and touchdown are comfortable, but the rollout is a bit rough. The runway is a mix of grass and hard-packed dirt, with lots of small ruts and rocks. Once down, we taxi to the clearing near the large building, which now is clearly identified as a tourist lodge. A solitary figure sits on the steps of the front deck waiting for us. My first hunch is that we are going to be asked to stay in the lodge rather than in our tent; my second guess is that we are going to be asked to leave.

I am wrong on both accounts. The man who approaches our airplane is glad to see us, but not for the reasons I expect.

"Hasn't been anyone here for weeks," says the caretaker. "No one has stayed at the lodge this year, but they pay me to take care of things. Good job, but it gets a bit lonely."

"Beautiful place," I respond. "But no tourists this year?"

"It's a fish camp," replies the caretaker. "This place was really busy last year, when the fishing was good. Charter planes from Vancouver used to come and go all the time."

"What happened?" I ask.

"They used to haul big trout out of here. But then they fished these lakes dry, so now the owners have a new lodge farther north. These days, the planes just fly on by."

The whole place has a sad feeling to it. A beautiful lodge sits empty on a gorgeous stretch of land nestled between two scenic lakes. Wouldn't tourists love this spot with or without fish?

"So what's going to happen to the lodge?" I ask.

"Don't know. The owners plan to keep it for a while. The fish will eventually come back, but not right away."

We're welcome to camp anywhere we desire, so we pick a spot on the opposite side of the runway in a grassy turnout. The tall weeds attract mosquitoes, and a noisy overabundance of grasshoppers jump all around our tent, *click-clicking* everywhere in sight. Insect heaven!

A wooden bridge behind our tent crosses the creek that connects Elkin Lake at the north end of the runway to Vedan Lake to the south. The creek looks perfect for trout. It's sad that the fish have disappeared from these waters. But maybe there are a few left, to reproduce and replenish the lakes.

I have no fishing rod or reel, but the airplane's survival kit has a small spool of nylon fishing line and two hooks. I prepare a pole, using a branch tied to the line. For bait, I use cheese along with grasshoppers that are leaping all around us. I climb down under the bridge and toss my line into the water.

Bam! – on my first awkward cast, a ten-inch trout hits the hook, and I quickly drag him out of the water. This place is just too perfect not to have a few remaining fish. I find another grasshopper for my hook – just reach out your hand, and a grasshopper is there. Then I throw my line back into the water. Meanwhile, Margy uses a similar setup (but without a pole) from above the bridge, sitting on the boards and fishing between the cracks.

Within a few minutes, we have five small but edible fish. How could the caretaker and the lodge's owners be so mistaken? Then the answer hits me – in a province full of big trout, small fish don't count in the grand scheme of big-time fish camps. Twin Lakes has been fished out. I am sampling on a small scale what once was and may be again in a few years.

* * * * *

Even planned destinations can bring unexpected discoveries. When flying into remote locations, it's often the norm.

Inuvik is our overnight destination, above the Arctic Circle and near the junction of the Yukon and Northwest Territories. Our Piper Arrow approaches the airport from the southwest (Yukon side), over-flying the marshy delta of the Mackenzie River. This river system is massive, the longest in Canada, flowing north to the Arctic Ocean from Great Slave Lake, with its tributaries starting much farther south at Lake Athabasca. The delta provides habitat for migrating snow geese and tundra swans and breeding habitat for other waterfowl. The estuary is a calving area for Beluga whales. A jumble of endless ponds and meandering streams pass below us.

Before landing at Inuvik Airport on this clear July day, I want to fly west along the Arctic Ocean shoreline. I explain my intensions to the Flight Service Station.

"Inuvik Radio, I'll be over-flying the airport at two thousand feet, continuing westbound along the coast to Shingle Point, to be followed by a course reversal and return to Inuvik for landing."

"Niner-niner-seven, understand. Let me know when you are inbound again."

"Roger, will report back inbound. Do you have time for a question?"

We are the only aircraft on frequency, so I doubt FSS is particularly busy.

"Sure, go ahead, nine-nine-seven."

"How far offshore is the sea ice this time of year?"

There is an extended pause, as I visualize the controller discussing my question with his fellow workers. It's probably a lot like locals everywhere, being so used to their environment that they don't pay much attention to things that interest tourists. After all, I live in California, 30 kilometres from Disneyland, but never go there.

"The ice is pretty far offshore this time of year. I'm looking at a satellite image that shows the nearest pack ice about 100 miles to the north."

The Arctic shoreline in this area is flat tundra, and summer temperatures can soar even higher than today's 20 degrees Celsius. I've watched First Nations children swim in the Arctic Ocean at Kugluktuk (Coppermine), east of here, on a 25-degree July afternoon, acting like it is a warm pond (it isn't!). It was at Kugluktuk that I finally accomplished my goal of camping on the shore of the Arctic Ocean on a blustery day with only a moderately chilly evening.

The flight westbound from Inuvik to Shingle Point is enchanting, and not only because of its wilderness beauty. This coastline is still dotted with remnants of the Cold War. Huge radomes of the DEW Line sit next to their adjoining electronics-crammed shacks. These are scary relics of the Distant Early Warning system designed to warn North America of inbound nuclear-tipped Russian missiles. Now mostly abandoned (a few are still operational for revised military purposes), the DEW Line facilities look ready for immediate reactivation. It's a reminder of how worldwide tensions have been reduced in recent years, regardless of localized conflicts that still make the headlines.

* * * * *

On a similarly warm summer day in the high Arctic, I pilot our Arrow along the shoreline, east of both Inuvik and Kugluktuk. Sheets of ice push into bays near the easternmost corner of the Northwest Territories. In the 100-kilometre stretch approaching Cambridge Bay, extensive slabs of sea ice appear below the airplane.

At Cambridge Bay, we refuel from a drum of gasoline, prearranged by a phone call. Margy pumps the gas while an Inuit airport worker assists. We use only half of the 50-gallon drum we have purchased, and offer the remaining fuel to the attendant. He explains in halting English that he would get in big trouble with his boss for accepting such a gift. As far as I know, the half-full drum was rolled to the side of the airport ramp, where it still sits with my name on it.

This remote airport on the Arctic Ocean exhibits a mix of modern technology and classic aviation. Boeing 737 jets use the dirt runway to bring residents to and from Cambridge Bay. A modern turboprop airliner sits side-by-side with a four-engine DC-6 workhorse from forty years ago.

In Cambridge Bay's small hotel, I read about musk oxen in a pamphlet that I find on a table beside the bed. These shaggy creatures were ancient neighbors of the extinct woolly mammoth, and I'm surprised to learn that the bison-like animals are permanent residents of this area. They don't migrate, although it's difficult to imagine any animal surviving in the Arctic tundra during the throes of winter. I'd love to see a live musk ox, but they aren't a sight you can expect to see by wandering around town.

As I've learned many times before, the best tours of remote areas are conducted in the company of local taxicab drivers. They know the area and are a storehouse of information. During an airport camping visit to Lac La Biche, Alberta, the taxi turned out to be the local ambulance, which worked well since no emergency calls were received during our ride.

At Cambridge Bay, a local taxi driver agrees to take us out onto the tundra, to look for musk oxen. But he's reluctant. He reminds us that these animals can be ornery when provoked. His implication is that the few tourists who ever set foot here are just the kind of people who provoke irritable animals.

A few miles north of town, he pulls his unmarked cab, a white station wagon, off to the side of the dirt road.

"Over there," he says, pointing out onto the tundra, past a rise in the terrain. "Be careful."

Is it the cab driver's sixth sense or his local knowledge of where musk oxen are most often found? In any case, this spot looks no different from any other area along this desolate road. Margy and I grab our cameras and trudge over the small ridge.

As soon as we crest the hill, the tundra spreads before us in all of its summer splendor. Except for a few small bushes, the treeless plain flows in all directions, right up to the horizon. A few small lakes, no larger than ponds, are scattered over the undulating terrain. The closest pond lies just below us, and at its shoreline stand two musk oxen.

I creep closer to get a good photo. The cab driver's warnings are in the back of my mind. But these shaggy animals look amazingly docile. Margy and I gaze down on one of the most unusual species in the world. *Snap-snap* goes the shutter, and we're out of there. No need to push our luck.

* * * * *

Lutselk'e (pronounced Loot-sell-kay) is another airport wedged between two lakes. Located in the Northwest Territories, this airstrip gets my camping attention because of its depiction in the *Flight Supplement*. The airfield diagram shows lots of open space and only two small buildings. The long, narrow runway lies on a thin strip of land that separates Great Slave Lake and Stark Lake, with Snowdrift River running alongside.

Inbound to Lutselk'e, I report my position on the airport's CARS frequency. This is a radio communication outlet that supplements the government's air traffic control system. CARS (Community Aerodrome Radio Station) provides an extension of the ATC system in remote locations. CARS doesn't control traffic, but it can relay clearances and provide weather data and information about traffic in the area.

The NDB (non-directional beacon) approach to Lutselk'e does not go well. It's a good thing the weather is relatively clear, because the needle of my ADF (automatic direction finder) swings wildly from side-to-side. After landing and parking the Arrow, I visit the CARS facility, a tiny office with a First Nations woman at a radio console. She isn't keen on my request to take her picture, so I snap it quickly.

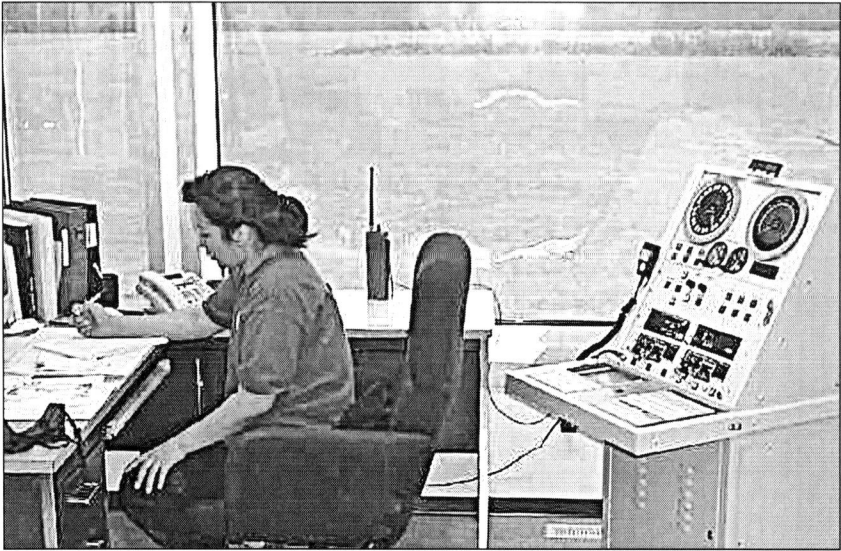

"Has anyone reported problems with the NDB?" I inquire.

The woman gives me a strange look and doesn't answer me. It seems she is avoiding my question or doesn't understand. Maybe she's mad at me for taking her picture. So I repeat my concern.

"My ADF needle was all over the place on the NDB approach. It could be my equipment, but it's been working fine at other airports."

The same strange stare, as if I've raised a question she doesn't want to acknowledge. Then she shrugs her shoulders and seems to relax a bit.

"Well, there's a problem with the beacon, but I'd rather not report it," she says. "Everybody knows the NDB is not working, so local pilots are just ignoring it."

Reporting standards for inoperative equipment are pretty straight-forward. If a pilot reports problems with a navigational aid, it's always taken seriously. Except, mysteriously, not here.

This CARS employee must know that I'm an American from her radio contact with me during the instrument approach. For some reason, she seems afraid to explain what is going on, maybe because I'm a pilot from the States.

I stand a few feet from her desk, while she runs her pen down a clipboard in front of her. She is more interested in the numbers on the sheet than me. The woman refuses to look directly at me, speaking more to the clipboard than to me.

"There's an osprey nest in the NDB tower, and they have babies," she finally says. It's a pleading tone.

A nest in the radio tower? I turn around and glance out the glass door. The NDB tower rises upward from the edge of the parking apron. Sure enough, a big nest covers the top of the radio tower. The source of NDB signal interference is now obvious.

"Cancel my report," I say. "Must be my equipment."

The CARS employee smiles and returns to her clipboard.

* * * * *

When Margy and I discovered Powell River, it was a eureka event that surpassed all other locations, even in the far north. It didn't grab our attention as suddenly as Anglemont or Twin Lakes, but that is part of the beauty of the place. It drew us in slowly, and then completely.

Margy and I camped on nearby Texada Island several times, but never ventured across the Malaspina Strait. When we finally discovered Powell River, it became our song of the sirens (minus the shipwrecks on the rocks). Powell River drew us in and never allowed us to venture far away again. The best destinations in life need not be sought – they will, somehow, find you.

◊ ◊ ◊ ◊ ◊ ◊

Chapter 5

Pacific Coastal

One evening, on a Pacific Coastal flight from Vancouver to Powell River, I meet Daniel. I've ridden with him before, watching him fly as first officer on this route. Tonight, as he leads the passengers to the Beechcraft 1900C sitting on the ramp at Vancouver's South Terminal, we strike up a conversation.

"You're instrument rated, I hope," I quip.

Daniel gives me an are-you-serious look, and then laughs: "I hope so. Someone will need to fly through these clouds tonight."

"Both Margy and I are pilots," I say, as we walk towards the aircraft. "We'd sure like to get our hands on the controls of an airplane like this."

"Sure, the captain and I will just sit in the back." He jokes.

We develop a friendly relationship right away, which is easy to do with someone like Daniel. As a flight instructor, I've worked with college students in the States who remind me of him – young, entirely devoted to flying, and living the dream.

After we land at Powell River, I tell Daniel about my books, and ask if he'd be willing to be interviewed for *Up the Airway*. His acceptance of this request leads to the fulfillment of one of my primary goals in writing this book – to include the contributions made by Pacific Coastal Airlines to BC's aviation community. The working environment of pilots up and down the coast is a mix of charter operations, intensely individual pilots, and Pacific Coastal.

My first interview with Daniel is scheduled for a day that coincides with an end-of-November snowstorm that cripples the south coast. Powell River's runway is closed by drifts, as plows try to clear a path for Pacific Coastal. The wind blows strong from the southeast, and visibility drops almost to zero. Daniel phones me from Vancouver to announce the not-so-surprising news.

"I won't be making it home to Powell River tonight," he says. "Sorry about the interview."

"No problem," I reply. "I bet you've been having fun the last few days."

This snowstorm, unusual for November, has wreaked havoc on the coast for three straight days, but tonight is the worst.

"Fun? You've got that right. You should have seen Williams Lake today. Couldn't find the runway until we were almost on the ground."

"I can imagine," I reply. "But you haven't been home in a while, have you?"

"Three days, one shirt," he remarks.

Where's my notebook? I knew I was interviewing the right guy.

* * * * *

Daniel provides me with an overview of Pacific Coastal's operating procedures, which are unique relative to airlines of any size. You don't maneuver in a mix of mountain and marine conditions in weather like this, unless you know how to be flexible. To be simultaneously flexible and safe is the real challenge, and Pacific Coastal has mastered both.

"Why pick on me?" asks Daniel. "I'm just the new guy around Pacific Coastal. There are some really experienced pilots you might want to talk to instead."

"I'll want to talk to them too. But I figure the new guy on the block can give me a good feel for how this airline operates."

"Okay, then let's go for it."

With that, Daniel gives me my first real insight into the way this Vancouver-based airline makes its mark on BC. With fourteen destinations and a diverse fleet of aircraft, Pacific Coastal started as a floatplane company. The floatplanes are still used as hub-and-spoke tools to get passengers to and from fish camps linked with remote locations like Bella Bella. The airline's bigger aircraft fly these same passengers back to Vancouver.

Daniel got his start at Pacific Coastal with only 1000 hours of flight time, near the minimum for new-hires. His initial hours were accumulated while flying with his father, a floatplane pilot who now flies Boeing 767s as an Air Canada captain. In Daniel's case, he brought considerable floatplane experience to Pacific Coastal from a charter floatplane company in Tofino, where he flew Cessna 185s and Beavers. Flying for a bush floatplane company provides amazing experience. Such flying is entirely under visual flight rules, often in grueling weather conditions. Daniel's destinations included challenging spots along the west coast of Vancouver Island. To make himself acceptable to Pacific Coastal, he needed to add a commercial certificate and a multi-engine instrument rating, which he completed at Boundary Bay Airport near Vancouver.

My own experiences at Boundary Bay make me realize that this is the ideal training environment for a career pilot. Tucked in close to Vancouver International in congested airspace, a pilot is forced to learn navigation and fast-paced air traffic control communications, skills particularly important for airline pilots.

After three summer seasons on floats, Daniel joined Pacific Coastal in 2006. They immediately threw him into the Shorts 360.

"No way – they started you in something smaller," I remark.

"The Shorts was it," says Daniel. "Lucky for me, it flies a lot like a Beaver."

"A mighty big Beaver, if you ask me," I suggest.

"An airplane is an airplane is an airplane," he replies. "Pull back and you go up, push forward and you go down."

Spoken like a kid who grew up with a yoke in his hand.

"But it's still a huge airplane. Funny looking too," I add.

You can't glance at a Shorts 360 without a bit of a laugh.

"The Shorts is a cool machine. Like a bus," observes Daniel. "But it has a wing almost identical to a Beaver, with similar struts and aileron counterweights sticking out – essentially a Beaver wing. It lumbers along, climbs slowly. It felt comfortable right away."

But there was a steep learning curve regarding air traffic control communications. A floatplane pilot's world is VFR, not the IFR world of airlines, with rapid-fire ATC communications during the entire flight.

"The huge thing for me was the radio work. I developed few radio skills flying out of Tofino. It's still my biggest challenge."

These days, Daniel flies the swifter looking Beech 1900C. He loves that airplane too.

"The 1900 is worlds apart from the Shorts. It's pressurized, fast, and you can go down and slow down at the same time. With the Shorts, you push the nose down and it speeds up quickly."

I ask about one of my main fears when flying in the coastal BC winter months: ice that can cause wings to rapidly loose their lift.

"Both the Shorts and 1900 use boots," notes Daniel, referring to the inflatable rubber boots used to break ice from the wing. "But the Shorts doesn't seem to care about ice. She slows down with ice but keeps on flying. The Shorts derives twenty percent of its overall lift from its fuselage."

How many aircraft can make this claim? The airplane may be ugly in profile, but it's an efficient flying machine.

The Beech 1900C doesn't carry ice as well, so it's necessary to use the boots carefully. The airplane has boots on the tail too, and heated props.

"With the 1900, we try to avoid ice on our trips into the interior. Sometimes, when there's ice in the forecast, we'll begin our climb-out from Vancouver by starting towards the west. We'll climb towards Comox and then double back over Vancouver to gain altitude before heading towards the brunt of the ice over the coastal mountains. With luck, we're above the clouds most of the way to Castlegar or Trail."

The Beech 1900 handles ice okay, but pilots have to treat it with respect. As Daniel says about the 1900C: "When we blow the boots, the ice comes off nicely."

I ask about Pacific Coastal destinations. Surely he has some favorites.

"Trail, when the weather is good. It's one of our newer destinations. Often we'll shoot the approach into Castlegar first, since Trail has no instrument approach, not even a beacon," meaning a non-directional radio beacon. "Then we'll fly down the valley to Trail, looking down on the ski run at Red Mountain. Simply beautiful!"

Airports on Pacific Coastal's list of destinations vary from the sophisticated ILS of Comox to the basic letdown at Bella Coola where you often need to descend over Anahim Lake and then fly down the valley to the airport. The road below is one of the most challenging switchbacks in BC, with a grade of 19 percent.

When I ask about his least favorite destination, Daniel doesn't hesitate an instant: "Victoria!" he says with a measure of disdain. "You're busy the whole time. You take off from Vancouver, and it's constant radio work all the way to landing." He pauses and then adds: "I'd rather not."

I understand the exasperation over such a short flight in busy airspace. It's easier to fly hundreds of kilometres than navigate a quick up-and-down, where there's too much happening in too little time.

Pacific Coastal is a unique airline in so many ways. Maybe that's why they continue to make a profit in a challenging industry and demonstrate such a superb safety record. Almost all airlines fly strictly IFR. But that's not efficient along the west coast of BC. Instead, Pacific Coastal flights normally begin with an IFR climb-out. If weather permits, the captain will often cancel IFR soon after takeoff and continue on a "company note," an internal VFR flight notification.

Many of the airline's destinations require a mix of IFR and seat-of-the-pants VFR flying. Over the years, Pacific Coastal has evolved from a bush company fleet of floatplanes to an IFR company with a wide variety of aircraft, and they maintain the efficiencies of both. It's an excellent selection of airplanes for the places and conditions in which Pacific Coastal flies.

And then, of course, there's GPS: "It changes everything," says Daniel.

All of Pacific Coastal's aircraft are GPS equipped. For the type of flying this airline does in all kinds of weather along the BC coast, the installation of GPS is one of the biggest safety improvements in recent years. Even the infamous NDB-DME approach into Powell River is wonderfully less exciting with a GPS receiver aboard as a backup. Most of the Beech 1900s carry a Garmin 430, the same reliable unit installed in my Arrow. You can't fly with this piece of equipment and not fall in love with it.

It's a different aviation world now. Flying has changed, but has lost none of its mystique and personal challenge. The more things change, the more they stay the same. Ask Pacific Coastal. Or simply meet a young airline pilot like Daniel.

* * * * *

Before Pacific Coastal came along, BC regional airlines were in a constant state of flux. The fast growth of regional airlines was exceeded only by the rate they went out of business. One of the most memorable was Air BC.

On a visit to Prince Rupert in 1994, I watched an Air BC British Aerospace 146 preparing to board passengers as we arrived in the Arrow. A path of huge duck footprints painted on the tarmac led the way from the airplane to the terminal, appropriate for Prince Rupert's wet climate. The British Aerospace 146 is the smallest airliner ever to be powered by four jet engines, not a particularly economical design. But it's an exciting airplane to see on the ramp.

Air BC formed in 1980 and became an Air Canada regional partner in 1987. The small airline consolidated with four other small airlines in 2001 to form Jazz, Air Canada's discount carrier.

Faded away, but not forgotten, you'll still find *Scare BC* scratched on the metal towel dispenser in the men's washroom at Powell River Airport. It's certainly not a just appraisal, but it shows the impression left by ever-changing regional carriers.

* * * * *

Daniel offers to give me a tour of the Beech 1900C on an upcoming Saturday, when a spare Pacific Coastal aircraft is parked all-day at Powell River, pre-positioned for the Sunday schedule. I call him on a mid-February morning to arrange our appointment. As usual, I open our cell phone conversation by asking him where he is. I expect him to be in the midst of a turnaround at Vancouver International.

"Tofino!" is his unexpected reply.

"What? On a Pacific Coastal flight or a vacation?"

"Days off," he announces.

In the background is a distant rumbling sound that could be the cell phone connection or waves crashing against the beach.

"Going surfing?" I ask.

This kid is the biggest surfing addict I've ever met (and I'm from California).

"I'm there right now. Just getting suited up."

That explains the rumbling sound in the phone. It's those huge waves on the west coast of Vancouver Island.

"Man, you're a real surfing nut. How big are the waves today?"

"Oh, about chest-high. Nice day for it."

Mid-February on the west coast of Vancouver Island. If you've been there, you can put Daniel's pronouncement of a nice day for surfing in perspective. It takes a special attitude to brave the bone-numbing cold of the winter North Pacific.

My tour of a Beech 1900C will have to wait.

One morning in March, I phone Daniel again. The phone rings several times before a hard-breathing voice comes on the line.

"Where are you?" I ask in my customary interrogation.

"Snowboarding. Whistler," he pants.

When he can't fly or ride the big waves, he can surf on top of snow.

"Got time to talk about a flying project?" I ask.

Background sounds this time betray the soft swishing of skis (or snowboards) over the snow.

"Not now," he says. "Gotta go!"

He hangs up promptly, but I'm not insulted. I picture Daniel's buddies dashing off in front of him, determined to beat him to the bottom of the slope. If it weren't for that dreaded on-reserve telephone call that might come in from Pacific Coastal, I bet he wouldn't even have answered his phone today. Surf or ski as much as you desire, but make sure you answer your phone by the fifth ring.

◊ ◊ ◊ ◊ ◊ ◊

Chapter 6

Up Victor 27

I've spent more time on Victor 27 than any other airway. Hop onto V27 near Santa Barbara and follow it along the California and Oregon coast all the way to Astoria. From there, it's a short jog inland to Olympia and then north to Bellingham, my regular stopover in Washington before entering Canada.

Those not familiar with my Piper Arrow seem surprised that I fly this route regularly in such a small aircraft. But Victor 27 is an easy ride in most seasons, with the Pacific Ocean moderating the weather conditions. Although low coastal clouds are common on this airway, I'll take stable stratus over cumulus instability any day. V27 reigns supreme as one of the smoothest routes in the world. Except, that is, during winter, when its northern reaches can be outrageously turbulent.

The most common question I'm asked about this route: "How long does it take?" The next most frequent question: "What does it cost?"

The first question is the easiest to answer. Los Angeles to Powell River takes eleven hours of flight time, although persistent headwinds or tailwinds can alter that standard by an hour either way. At least two fuel stops are required. Santa Rosa (just north of San Francisco) and Astoria are often places where I refuel, since they are strategically located near the limits of the Arrow's fuel range and provide quick turnaround service.

When summer daylight hours are long, I've often flown from Los Angeles to Powell River in a single day, including a lunch stop at Astoria and Customs in Nanaimo. But that's a long day of flying, so a camping destination along the way is a welcome break. One of my favorite overnight camping spots is Siletz Bay (Gleneden Beach) in northern Oregon.

Arrival at Siletz Bay is normally accompanied by gusty afternoon wind, due to the airport's location near the beach. The airport sits in a transition zone where the sea breeze collides with inland convection. Prevailing winds usually favor a landing to the north on Runway 35.

Final approach at Siletz Bay is seldom routine. Gusty winds lurk in the clear-zone for Runway 35 that extends a half-kilometre from the threshold. Large trees bordering the approach path form a sure setup for wind shear. In such gusts, it's best to increase your approach speed to avoid an aerodynamic stall. On a short runway like this, a careful trade of higher landing speed for longer landing roll is necessary, easily handled in the Arrow. A sideslip approach works well, with the yoke into the crosswind, opposite rudder, and two notches of flaps.

Siletz Bay is a beautiful airport and a great place to camp next to your airplane. Once settled in, it's a quick walk across the street to enjoy a great dinner at the Side Door Cafe.

The Arrow is always heavily loaded on this route, so particular attention is needed on this relatively short runway. With proper technique, landing is never a problem, but takeoff deserves special consideration. Arriving with a reduced fuel load helps, and an early morning departure with cool temperatures contributes to good takeoff performance. Once airborne, it's a short hop to Astoria for gas, if northbound, or Newport when southbound.

* * * * *

The second question ("What does it cost?") is tougher. The expense of a flight from Los Angeles to Powell River varies considerably, since you really should include accumulated expenses for maintenance and other costs that are spread throughout the year. The simplest (though inaccurate) answer is expressed in terms of the amount of fuel, since that is the most immediate operational cost. But that begs the real question.

My simplified answer: Fuel costs for a small airplane carrying two people on a long flight are typically a bit less than airfare for an airline on the same route.

But there are always other costs incurred by airplane owners – lots of other costs. For example, consider one flight along Victor 27 that I'll always remember as the flight involving the "engine change from hell."

*****

Southbound to Los Angeles for a University of Southern California football game (and other less important things) in late September, I watch towering cumulus clouds to my left growing into a line of thunderstorms. The ocean's onshore flow of marine air protects Victor 27 from land-based storm clouds. A few miles inland, the Coastal Range marks the dividing line between cruising tranquility and uncomfortable turbulence.

It's been a smooth trip, with a fuel stop ahead at Crescent City and then the long ride down the length of California. The weather looks terrific.

Climbing out of Crescent City to an assigned IFR cruising altitude of seven thousand feet, Margy maneuvers the Arrow while I talk to ATC and setup the navigation receivers. We've just entered the northern tip of California, which marks the halfway point for this trip. Five hours of flying lies ahead of us.

The climb seems sluggish, so I glance at the airspeed and vertical speed indicators, comparing their readings. This airspeed is normal for a best-rate climb (103 miles per hour), but we are climbing at only 300 feet per minute. That's a lower rate of climb than expected, although the contributing factors are complex. Power settings are normal (25 inches of manifold pressure and 2500 RPM), but our aircraft is heavy, and it's a warm afternoon. Weight and temperature have a big effect on rate of climb.

Margy is my constant source of feedback regarding aircraft performance. She knows this airplane well and speaks up when she's troubled. I glance at Margy as she adjusts the pitch trim – she seems unconcerned.

We pass Fortuna VOR just before leveling at seven thousand feet. It has been a slow struggle up to cruising altitude. Still, all seems relatively normal for a heavily loaded Arrow in a hot air mass. Then I hear a slight hesitation in the engine.

It grabs my attention. But the cockpit is a noisy place, and sound-canceling headsets cover much of the engine noise. Just moving your head quickly can produce a change in engine sound. What I think I've heard is probably not significant. In fact, it may be meaningless. I steal a quick look at Margy, and it's apparent she has not heard anything unusual.

Margy makes final cruise adjustments with the prop lever and the mixture control. Then she reaches down to tweak the rudder trim, giving it a twist to the left to account for the slight change in propeller torque at cruising speed. You don't bother with trim tabs when you suspect an engine problem.

I check the engine instruments, including the exhaust gas temperatures (EGT) for all four cylinders. I'd rather check cylinder head temperatures (CHT), but that portion of the indicator is inoperative today. It's a fickle split gauge that shows EGT and CHT on the same instrument. Sometimes both temperatures are displayed, sometimes only one. Right now, I can only view EGT, with the CHT needle lifeless at the bottom of the gauge.

Oil pressure and temperature are normal. Most important of all, Margy is now settled back in her seat, a critical indicator of engine performance. Then it happens again.

This time, Margy stirs in her seat. Out of the corner of my eye, I notice the tachometer drop 50 RPM and then immediately return to normal. It happens fast.

"Did you hear that?" says Margy, in a voice of concern.

"Yuh, I heard it. Saw it too – on the tachometer."

"What do you think?" she asks, sounding calmer now that the moment has passed.

"Don't know. Sounds like a momentary surge. Maybe the prop governor is hunting a bit."

The constant-speed prop on the Arrow is supposed to keep the RPM steady in cruise, even when the pilot adjusts the throttle. It's a more efficient system than the fixed-pitch prop on smaller aircraft. It's also more complex, incorporating a prop governor that hydraulically adjusts the angle of the blades. When something goes astray in this system, the tachometer may be the first sign of trouble.

"Reminds me of that broken oil control ring on the way to Phoenix," Margy proclaims.

She may not be a mechanical expert, but Margy has a memory of engine incidents that is uncanny. She is right – the hesitation and accompanying sound is exactly like an incident that occurred 200 flight hours ago. At eleven thousand feet over Arizona, we broke an oil control ring, an unusual engine malfunction that caused us to return from Phoenix on an airliner. We've always had great luck with on-the-road repairs, getting unexpectedly high priority over local aircraft. Mechanics seem to take a particular delight in assisting out of town pilots in distress. Still, the Phoenix repairs were costly, including an airline flight back to Los Angeles and then a return flight to retrieve the airplane the next week.

Today, at seven thousand feet, things settle down again, and I make a slight adjustment to the mixture control, enriching the fuel-air ratio. This results in a reduction of engine temperature that seems to help, because the disturbing hesitation does not happen again all the way home.

This is not unusual in the operation of aircraft. Problems come, and sometimes they are significant. But sometimes it is just one of those things, as minor as a bubble of water in the fuel system. All settles down, and we arrive in Los Angeles before sunset.

* * * * *

The next day, I refuel the Arrow at Brackett Field (Pomona), in preparation for a flight to Tucson. This is the real reason for the timing of our trip, a football game between USC and the University of Arizona. Since it will be an early takeoff the following morning, I decide to perform a preflight inspection now. The result is an alarming discovery – only two quarts of oil remain in the eight-quart engine.

This becomes a very expensive football game. With our plans to fly the Arrow to Arizona canceled, we take an airliner to Phoenix the next day and rent a car for the trip to Tucson. We also arrange for an expensive overhaul of an engine only 550 hours old. The good news is that USC wins the game, after a second half comeback.

* * * * *

It takes several days to determine the cause of the oil loss and its relationship to the in-flight conditions over northern California. A bad cylinder is suspected, but it's difficult to determine which one. Compression in all of the combustion chambers is normal, yet the spark plugs foul during ground runs. Randy, maintenance director at the local aircraft repair shop, elects to remove and inspect the cylinder that seems most suspect, based on his analysis of the fouled plugs. He picks the correct one.

Randy finds a broken oil control ring, just as Margy deduced. Unfortunately, it is a different cylinder than the previous incident in Arizona. Oil control ring malfunctions are almost unheard of, and two such failures in different cylinders are beyond coincidental. Overheat and detonation are suspected, and further engine damage is probable. In a nutshell, this engine no longer has our confidence. The oil control ring could be replaced, but the engine may be damaged elsewhere. We don't have to look much closer to find more evidence.

With the damaged oil control ring and piston removed, Randy peers into the crankcase and finds small flakes of metal in the interior of the engine, along with visible damage to lobes of the camshaft. At only a quarter of the normal operating time between major overhauls, this engine goes to the engine shop for a complete teardown.

An electronic ignition system installed on the engine at the previous overhaul is the suspected culprit. Although such technology has been standard on automobile engines for decades, almost all small aircraft engines use old-fashioned magnetos for ignition. Magnetos are extremely reliable, but electronic ignition provides improved power efficiency. We (Randy, the engine overhaul shop, and I) suspect the electronic ignition system as the cause of this engine damage. The decision is unavoidable – overhaul the engine and switch back to traditional magnetos. It's a difficult decision to make, since deactivation of the electronic ignition system and installation of new magnetos will be very expensive.

While the engine overhaul is in progress, N41997 gets an upgrade to her avionics equipment. A replacement intercom is installed and an IFR-certified GPS is added. The older VFR-only GPS remains in the aircraft as a backup, but the new Garmin 430 is a major improvement. A bright and colorful moving map will be a wonderful enhancement. Included with the installation are a new VOR and an upgraded communication radio, so this is a major cockpit renovation.

* * * * *

Margy and I return from Canada in December to fly the Arrow back north for the winter. Of course, this is a reversal of the normal "snowbird" route, but the aircraft's legal residence is now in Bellingham, and its hangar is in Powell River. We need the airplane wherever we are, and increasingly that is in Powell River or Bellingham.

When we arrive in Pomona, the engine overhaul is complete, but its installation back onto the aircraft has not yet begun. The engine sits on the floor in Randy's hangar. In a box next to the engine are expensive components from the old engine, now usable only as coffee table decorations. Margy picks out two old pistons, and I select the damaged camshaft. The rest of the old parts go into the trash.

Putting an engine back onto an airplane requires expertise and patience. With Christmas approaching, Randy has a full hangar and not enough working time allocated for his mechanics. Two other airplanes await their new engines, while a twin-engine charter aircraft sits on jacks and a Bonanza is in the midst of a major airframe refurbishment. All of the mechanics have their assignments, and things cannot fall further behind schedule. So Randy takes the Arrow's engine installation on himself.

Having the boss install the engine is a pleasant surprise, but there are disadvantages. Whenever the phone rings, it's usually for Randy. His employees need supervision too, so he works on my airplane whenever he can. It doesn't speed up the process to have me constantly looking over Randy's shoulder. My interest in the installation (along with my endless questions) is enough to make any mechanic explode. However, Randy takes it all in stride.

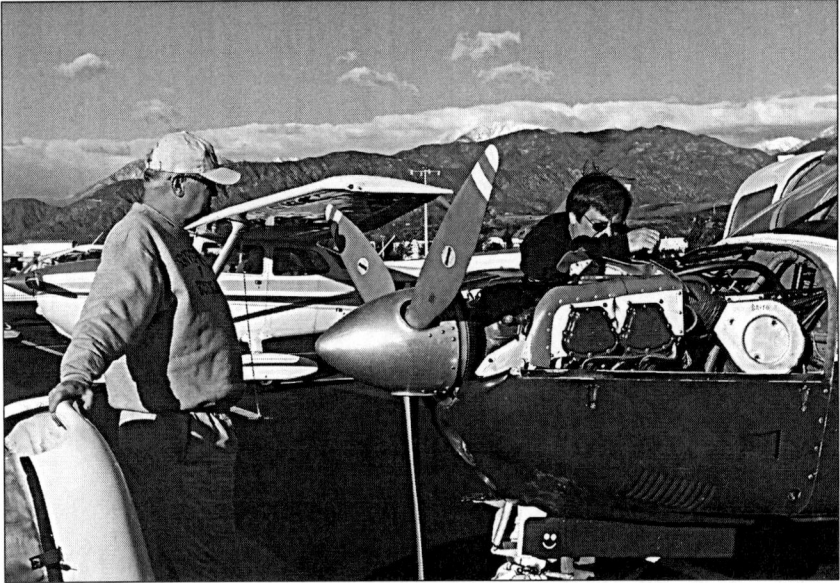

Meanwhile, I scrutinize the daily weather maps. Storms move down quickly from the Gulf of Alaska, swooping along the BC coast into Washington and Oregon. The trailing edges of these frontal systems drop down through central California and stall out. Los Angeles basks in sunshine, day after day, with daytime temperatures near 20 degrees C.

The storms along the Pacific Northwest are lined up far out over the ocean, with no relief in sight. I wait for a weather window, but breaks between storms are too narrow to fly a small aircraft all the way to the Canadian border. It's a mute point. I don't have an engine.

Finally, the newly installed engine receives its first ground run. Then Randy turns the aircraft over to me for a test flight.

Even with Margy aboard to assist, the first flight is a hectic one. It's also short, just long enough to get engine temperatures up to normal. We monitor the gauges closely, but this is also the first test of the new avionics equipment. I turn on the new GPS and run a few quick checks, though most of my concentration is on the engine, which performs flawlessly.

Back on the ground, Randy removes the cowl and inspects the engine for leaks. A tiny puddle of oil sits on the metal shelf right below the oil filter. Randy uses a wrench to snug up the filter, gives the engine another thorough inspection, and signs off the paperwork.

This same afternoon, an amazing coincidence occurs. A brief weather window has opened. The most recent storm along the coast has moved inland, and there is a gap before the next frontal system moves ashore. If TV's Weather Channel is correct, the window will be open for two full days. We take advantage of the opportunity, load the airplane, and prepare for an early departure the next morning.

* * * * *

We're airborne at 7:02 am, winging upward to join Victor 27. The sun is just rising in the east, advertising clear skies. We plan to take advantage of all the daylight hours possible, maybe even making it all the way to Bellingham before dark. There will be no stopping except for fuel and restroom breaks.

Our first scheduled stop is Monterey, a conservative flight distance for a new engine. This first leg will be conducted VFR, so we can fly low, an important part of the engine break-in process. During the first few hours, it's important to keep power settings high, and that's impossible to achieve at higher IFR altitudes and the accompanying thinner air. So we elect to fly VFR and low.

As we climb out of Los Angeles, Margy flies while I navigate, talk to ATC, and try to learn the intricacies of the new avionics equipment. One of our priorities is to certify the GPS for IFR on the trip north. I plan to accomplish this by logging the electronically-derived coordinates of the runways we use along the way. So far, I can't even find the display screen that contains our latitude and longitude.

After reaching our selected VFR cruising altitude of 4500 feet (low enough for proper engine break-in), I contact ATC to establish radar traffic advisories. Meanwhile, Margy turns on the flight director. But nothing happens – not even an *On* light.

No flight director also means no autopilot. And the DME isn't working either. Both of these control panels sit immediately adjacent to the new GPS and intercom. With so much avionics installation activity in this part of the instrument panel, it's not unexpected to find a few related problems. But it would have been nice to find them before we are headed 1800 kilometres away from our avionics shop.

Of course, we could have turned this equipment on for a brief trial during the test flight yesterday, and then it could have been fixed by the shop immediately, but our attention was on the engine and new GPS. The avionics problem may only be a connector that is not properly attached, and there will be an avionics shop in Bellingham. But it would have been nice to have a fully operational flight director for the trip north.

North of Santa Barbara, we climb to 6500 feet to clear the rising terrain ahead. Fifteen minutes later, past the Santa Ynez Mountains, we drop back down to 4500 feet.

I scan the CHT gauge, evaluating all four cylinders every few minutes. I also spend some time with the new GPS, jumping from instructions in the manual to the various setup screens on the moving map display. It's great to have the older Northstar GPS as a cross-reference for the new unit. No matter how much you trust a piece of equipment, it doesn't hurt to have a backup. And I can use the two units to set up more waypoints and prepare for the next segment of the route. It's a lot like having a second communication radio (as all IFR aircraft do) to prepare for the next sector of airspace.

"Loadmeter seems low," says Margy.

I glance over to the pilot's side of the instrument panel to check the loadmeter. This is a left-zero ammeter that registers the actual load on the alternator. Normally, I expect to see the needle near the center of the gauge, indicating that a large amount of electrical equipment is in use. Now I see a full-left indication.

"Has it been that far to the left since the engine change?" I ask.

"I'm not sure. I know it was reading higher during the engine run-up, both yesterday and today."

Run-up is an opportunity to check the health of the electrical system. We routinely recycle the alternator switch to check the loadmeter at the beginning of each flight. During flight, Margy keeps an eye on this gauge, since it is difficult to see from my side of the aircraft.

"I think it has been riding a bit lower during cruise than before the engine change, but not this low," Margy adds.

Things like this happen when you change an engine. The oil pressure gauge, previously considered normal when positioned one needle-width into the green arc is now a bit higher. It's to be expected. The lower loadmeter reading may be related to the new radios. Modern radios consume a lot less current than older ones.

I turn on the landing light to see if the loadmeter flickers. It doesn't, even though the landing light consumes a lot of power. Then I flick on the pitot heat, another energy consuming item. Once again, the needle doesn't budge.

"Keep an eye on it, but I think it's okay," I instruct.

Famous last words.

Why didn't I elect to recycle the split master switch? Good question, and I have no good answer. It's simple to reset the alternator field circuit by a quick recycle of the switch, but I ignore it. The air is clear, the ride smooth, and there are no problems – so it seems. But trouble is brewing inside the alternator, which is probably already dead. We are now on battery power, and the loadmeter is telling us so. But we ignore the warning signs.

Over Big Sur, Margy begins our descent into Monterey with instructions from the radar approach controller to follow the coastline for a right base leg to Runway 10R. ATC hands us off to the control tower. My first radio call to the tower results in a loud squeal in my headset.

"November four-one-niner-niner-seven. If that's you calling, that radio is totally unreadable with a loud squeal in the background."

My new communications radio has let me down, or is it worse than that? I switch to the backup radio and try transmitting again. The squeal is still there.

"Niner-niner-seven, if you hear me, you're cleared to land on Runway One-Zero Right. There is traffic…"

The controller's instructions go abruptly dead, the squeal is gone, the bright GPS display goes blank, and all the other cockpit digital displays disappear. It's a total electrical failure. I finally reach down to the master switch and recycle the alternator side of the split switch, but I'm an hour too late. The alternator failed somewhere near Santa Barbara, and the battery has now followed suit.

But it's a clear morning, Monterey Airport looms large in the windshield, and we're cleared to land. It's really no big deal, but this engine break-in flight has quickly become a logistics nightmare. An alternator failure is not directly related to an engine overhaul (the old alternator was reused during the engine change), but now we have a failed flight director, a malfunctioning DME, and a totally inoperative electrical system. It gets worse.

Margy asks me to take the airplane for the landing, since I supposedly have more experience in situations like this. Turning onto final approach over the harbour, I lower the landing gear. I feel the normal deceleration as the gear comes down, but no gear-down lights appear. Without an electrical system, the three green down-and-locked lights aren't expected to illuminate. The gravity-override gear extension system has obviously done its job (I felt the drag, didn't I?), but what if the landing gear is not fully down and locked? Normal gear extension in this airplane is through an electrically-activated (hydraulically-driven) pump. With this pump inoperative, the gravity freefall of the wheels may not exert enough force to activate the over-center mechanism that locks the gear down. There are three independent wheels that must lock down accordingly. Without the green down-and-locked lights, it's anybody's guess.

"Go around!" exclaims Margy.

She raises her voice to be heard in the cockpit – no electricity, no intercom. Margy sees the same thing I see – no green lights. I'm thinking exactly the same as she is (go around), but I continue to swoop low over Runway 10R, hoping the battery will provide one last flicker of power to the green lights. Over the runway numbers, I finally push the throttle forward to begin the missed approach. The Arrow climbs slowly, since it is heavy and the gear is down, with no hope of retraction without electrical power.

The control tower has no idea why I am executing a missed approach, since they are unable to communicate with me. I visualize them clearing jet traffic around me, watching my every move and waiting for me to get safely on the ground. Inside the cockpit, I'm struggling with the climb, while making a left turn to clear the hills on the inland side of the airport. With my right hand on the yoke, I reach behind my seat with my other hand, fumbling with my flight bag, trying to find the portable VHF radio. I feel the antenna and use it to pull the small radio from the bag.

We climb upward and turn left, now on the downwind leg for Runway 10R. I ask Margy to take the airplane, while I turn on the portable radio (full volume for the noisy cockpit) and tune it to the control tower frequency. I hold the microphone close to my mouth and yell more than talk.

"Monterey Tower, this is Arrow niner-niner-seven on a handheld radio. How do you hear?"

"You're loud and clear, niner-niner-seven. Go ahead."

"We've experienced complete electrical failure and do not have landing gear down-and-locked lights in the cockpit. Request you verify our gear is down."

"Nine-nine-seven, roger. Your landing gear appears to be down. I see all three wheels. Are you declaring an emergency?"

This is standard ATC phraseology. The tower controller can see wheels extending from the aircraft, but he has no way to confirm the gear is locked down. Thus, he states the gear "appears to be down." But it's a relief to know that he sees all of our wheels. Now if only they are locked in place.

"Negative emergency." I reply.

I don't feel it is necessary to roll the fire trucks, but it will be an adrenaline-producing touchdown.

"Roger, niner-niner-seven. You're cleared to land on Runway One-Zero Right."

"I'll keep it nice and gentle during touchdown," I tell Margy. "Here, monitor the radio, and I'll land the airplane."

"We're okay," she replies confidently, as she relinquishes the controls to me and jams the small radio against her ear.

She knows exactly what "appears to be down" means.

"Could be expensive," I say with a forced laugh.

There is nothing more to do than make the smoothest landing possible and not take it too seriously. Gear-up landings are rare, and they seldom result in injuries. But damage can be extensive. First there are the belly sparks as the rear of the aircraft contacts the concrete, and then the prop strikes the runway. The wings (containing fuel) come down last, but they are designed to contain the gas in such a situation.

If you want to worry about expenses, consider the regulations regarding propellers that hit solid pavement. A prop strike is automatic cause for engine overhaul, since the crankshaft could be damaged. Our recent engine overhaul came prematurely at 550 hours. Now there may be another one required after a mere 3 hours of flight. It's worth a laugh, to prevent crying.

The landing and rollout are a non-event, except for a tremendous sense of relief in the cockpit. I use the handheld radio to thank the tower controller.

"Just part of our job. Taxi to parking on this frequency. I hope your day gets better."

It couldn't get much worse.

The reality is that both Margy and I anticipate what lies ahead with a sense of adventure. That probably sounds sadistic, but we've often found that some of our greatest adventures in life begin with an unexpected layover. Weather is the normal cause of such deviations, but unscheduled maintenance is a close second. Somehow this will work out fine.

At the local maintenance shop, we're referred to Larry. Immediately, we can tell we've come to the right place. Larry is the director of maintenance, juggling a hangar full of airplanes in various stages of repair. His crew is a friendly group of mechanics who are spurred on by Larry's get-it-done leadership style. We get top priority in the repair schedule (again, moving ahead of the routine maintenance), and soon Larry's troubleshooting confirms we need a new alternator. Getting one means waiting until 10 am the next day for the priority shipment to arrive.

* * * * *

The alternator arrives on schedule and is installed quickly. All that is required is a final operational check. This, of course, requires starting the engine.

But it won't start. Larry fights with the starting procedure and then turns it over to me. Sometimes fuel injected aircraft engines can be fickle during startup, but it's hard to accept that a mechanic as experienced as Larry would have trouble with this Arrow. I crank away for a few minutes and finally get the engine running – barely. It struggles to warm up, chugging away on two cylinders, then three, and finally all four. But then the engine smooths out nicely. The alternator checks out fine, so it's time to shutdown and agonize over what has caused the rough start. But the engine won't stop.

The engine continues to run when I throttle back and pull the mixture control to idle-cutoff. The 3-hour-old engine stutters along, refusing to quit, until I advance the throttle far forward to force an overly lean mixture. As the engine finally shuts down, a shaking vibration and a final spurt of power get my attention. Nothing could be worse for engine break-in than this rough start and shaky shutdown.

One thing is fixed (alternator), and a new problem has developed. Larry scratches his head and adjusts the fuel control cable. The next start is no smoother, and the shutdown equally brutal.

I phone Randy and discuss the situation. I'd rather report that we're safely on the ground in Bellingham. Instead, we are still in southern California, and the new engine won't start or stop properly. Over the phone, Larry and Randy ponder the possibilities. Two superior mechanics are simultaneously stymied by the conditions we have encountered.

Larry keeps at it all afternoon, adjusting the fuel-air mixture setting, and checking the spark plugs and fuel injector lines. Finally, he finds the problem – the mixture control idle-cutoff mechanical stop is out of adjustment. It was fine for the original ground runs at home, as well as my first local test flight. Somehow, the star fasteners that secure the plastic-sheathed mixture control cable have slipped out of position, and the engine is not going to idle-cutoff. That explains the situation – the engine is not fully starved of fuel at shutdown. During starts, the rich mixture setting allows the fuel pump to direct extra gas into the cylinders, flooding the plugs and preventing a smooth start.

Once Larry secures the cable against the mechanic stop, all is well again. The engine starts, runs, and shuts down like a normal aircraft engine. But now the day is over, the sun has set, and the two-day weather window has closed. According to the forecast, there could be another brief weather opportunity later this week.

So we settle in for two more nights. Margy and I make the best of it. I use my laptop computer in the hotel, finalizing page setup for my next book. I take an occasional break to study the manual for the new GPS. If we ever get airborne, I'll be an expert with the new equipment. Meanwhile, Margy attends to her school consulting projects.

The rain moves in. Farther north, the coast has cleared, but it will not remain that way for long. As soon as the sky clears in Monterey, we will be ready to go. Meanwhile, our airplane sits in the maintenance hangar, awaiting her next adventure.

* * * * *

At 7:30 the next morning, Margy does the engine run-up, while I set the GPS screen for "current position" to record its accuracy on the runway. Margy is concerned with this departure. This series of mechanical problems has caused her to question the overall health of the new engine. I know she'll be more comfortable once we're airborne.

"Stop being grumpy," I quip as we await our takeoff clearance.

"I'm not grumpy," she replies. "Just a bit nervous."

"I know, but it'll all be okay in a few minutes."

It's always that way. Usually any anxiety either of us have about a particular flight disappears the moment the engine is running. Today it may take a bit longer. Zooming upward through crystal clear skies is bound to help. And it does.

We're up and away, climbing under the guidance of ATC radar vectors to intercept Victor 27. We're on an IFR flight plan, but the minimum enroute altitudes (MEAs) in this area are low. We've been assigned 5000 feet, a perfect altitude for engine break-in. We'll be able to stay low for the first 100 miles, as we parallel the coastline just offshore from San Francisco. Later, as we approach the higher terrain north of Santa Rosa, we'll need to climb. But for now we fly through smooth, stable air along the coastline, with a scheduled fuel stop at Arcata in northern California.

I glance at the loadmeter regularly, the needle now riding comfortably in the normal range. I play with the GPS, dialing in waypoints and investigating the abundance of navigational screens. Approaching Mendocino, we receive our instructions to climb to 6000 feet. Margy is flying, and I'm having fun with ATC communications and setting up the navigational waypoints.

"Let's change our destination to Crescent City," I suggest. "It'll be a quicker fuel stop."

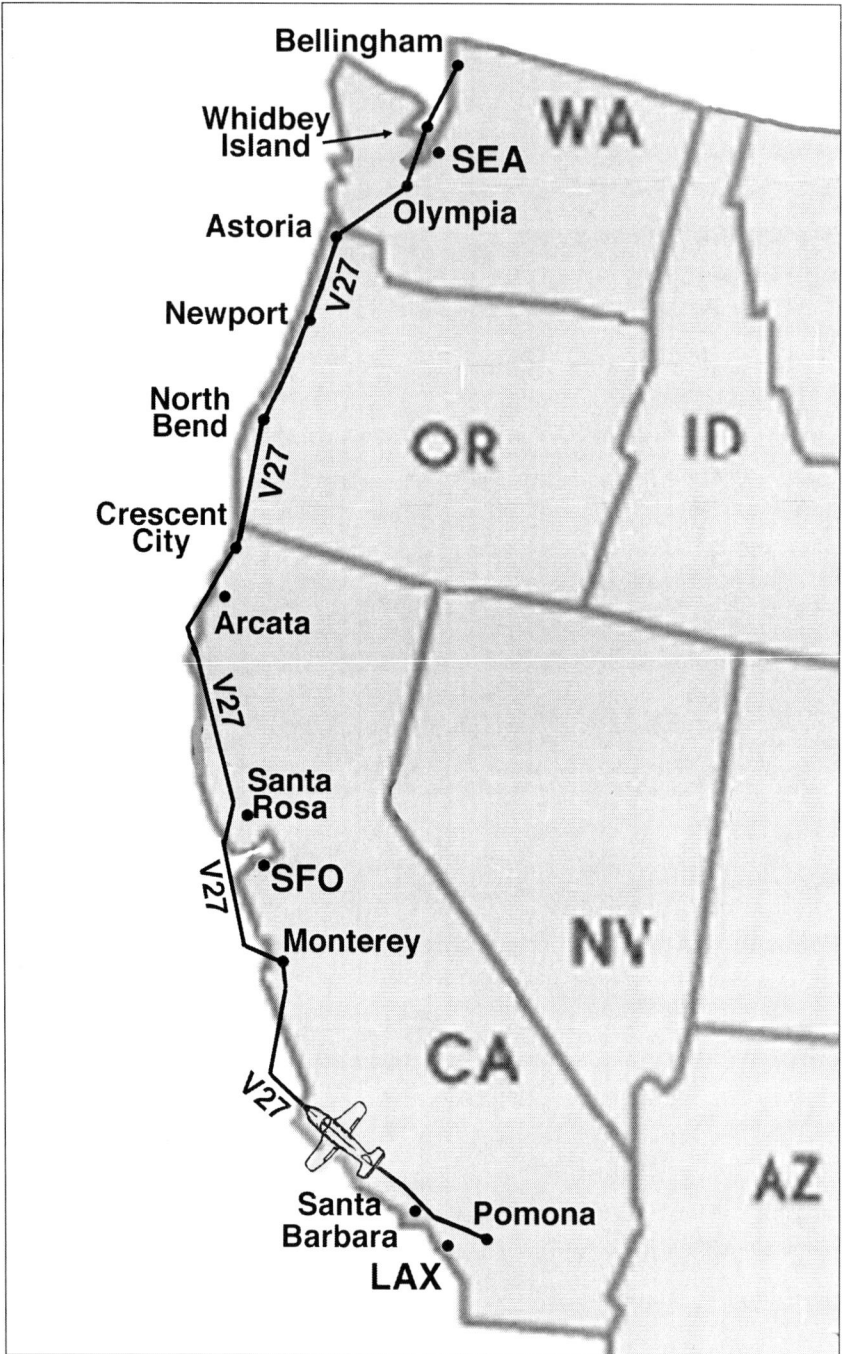

Up Victor 27

We know the airports along V27 well, and Crescent City will save us a few minutes as a gas stop. With the next storm already moving steadily towards the coast, even a little saved time will help.

"Sounds good," agrees Margy.

I call Oakland Center and arrange the change in destination. It's a simple process.

"November four-one-niner-niner-seven is now cleared to the Crescent City Airport via present position, Victor two-seven, direct. Maintain six thousand."

I read back the clearance, and we settle in for a leisurely trip up the coast in perfect flying conditions. When it goes good, as it does most of the time, it goes really good. Regardless of the challenges of this "engine change from hell," we are content with the outcome. Flying is like that – there is no way to compute the actual cost of flying. For us, the value of the experience outweighs the outrageous price tag.

Margy makes the landing at Crescent City, while I snap photos on final approach as waves crest over the rocks below. These giant breakers are associated with the endless winter storms that roar across the northern California coast this time of year. From this spot at the tip of California, we can see the spectacular Oregon coastline stretching northward in front of us.

The refuel goes quickly, although we take some extra time to remove the top cowl to check on the oil leak that has plagued the new engine since its first test flight, now six hours behind us. Randy tightened the oil filter, thinking it was the source of the seep. Larry saw oil again on the same ledge below the filter, and thought the source of leak might be the thermostatic control valve called the "Veratherm." He tightened the valve, but after an extensive engine run, a small amount of oil appeared again on the metal ledge. Safe, but on the must-fix-soon list.

Now, after this first leg of flight since Monterey, a small amount of oil has dripped down onto the nose tire while it was tucked inside the wheelwell during flight. I wipe down the tire so we can monitor the situation. I've seen such leaks before, and they are seldom a matter of concern relative to safety. A small leak can make an oily mess. We'll ask the shop at Bellingham to investigate further.

* * * * *

From Crescent City, we fly north along V27 to North Bend and then Newport. We watch a wall of high clouds slide inland, but the volcanic peaks to the east stick up into the sunshine. It's only along the coast where the weather window has started to close in. Mount Hood and Saint Helens still bask in the sun, providing a spectacular vista.

At Astoria, we refuel at the self-service pump. There is more oil on the nose wheel, but I decide not to wipe it off, leaving it as additional evidence to aid the mechanic in Bellingham. Margy just nods when I point to the oil on the tire and tell her why I am not wiping it clean. By now, we both feel comfortable with this new engine. We're relaxed and ready to finish the trip before the sun sets in Bellingham.

Margy performs the takeoff while I operate the radios and monitor CHT and oil pressure. We depart VFR to speed things along, picking up our IFR clearance in flight as we climb out of 3000 feet. Now we are headed inland to Olympia and then north to Bellingham, off Victor 27 for the first time today. Seattle Center issues our clearance five miles northeast of Astoria.

"November four-one-nine-nine-seven is cleared to the Bellingham Airport via direct Olympia, Victor one-six-five, as filed. Climb and maintain five thousand, squawk code four-six-two-three."

We cruise over Olympia and turn left towards the intricate channels created by patterns of ocean and islands in Puget Sound. To the west, the Olympic Mountains stick up towards the darkening, high overcast clouds. To the east, Mount Rainier rises beyond Tacoma. Farther ahead, Mount Baker is now visible in the distance, yellow-capped in the setting sun.

Below us, scattered stratus clouds are moving in, while the dark layer above continues to thicken, threatening rain. But we've got it made now.

The last few minutes of this flight are a whirlwind of ATC hand-offs: Seattle Approach Control assigns us to Whidbey Island military controllers who quickly turn us over to Victoria Terminal (a short jog through Canadian airspace). Victoria clears us for a visual approach and hands us off to Bellingham Tower. Eight hours of flying, two fuel stops, and who knows how much it all costs. But to us, this adventure has been priceless.

◊ ◊ ◊ ◊ ◊ ◊ ◊

Center-of-Book Illustrations

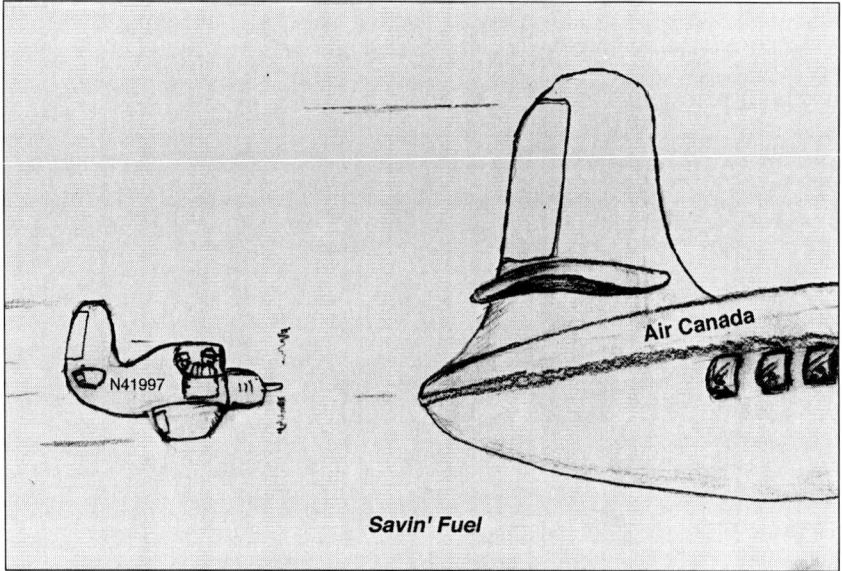

N41997

Air Canada

Savin' Fuel

Twin Beech Floatplane at the Shinglemill, Powell Lake (2007)

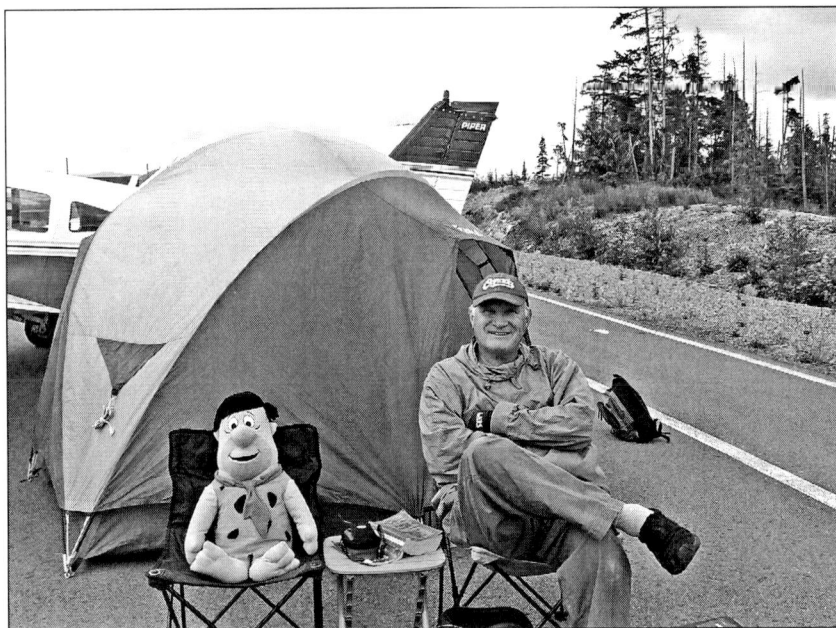

Camping at Bella Bella Airport, Campbell Island

Offshore View of Powell River Runway 09

Short Final, Powell River Runway 09

Oceanview "Smarties" – Green, Red, Red, Yellow

Powell River Airport and City

Sechelt Floatplane Base, Lower Sunshine Coast

Chilliwack Airport, BC

Siletz Bay, Oregon

Camping at Siletz Bay

Hope Airport, BC

Camping at Hope

Texada Island Airport, BC

Texada Shoreline is Accessible from the Airport by a Short Trail

Brackett Airport – Home Airfield in Southern California

Arrow N41997 Landing at Kern Valley Airport, California

Bella Coola, BC

Watson Lake, Yukon

Lutselk'e Firefighting Aircraft, Northwest Territories

Camping at Chehalis-Centralia Airport, Washington

Hudson's Hope, BC

Prince Rupert Flight Service Station, BC

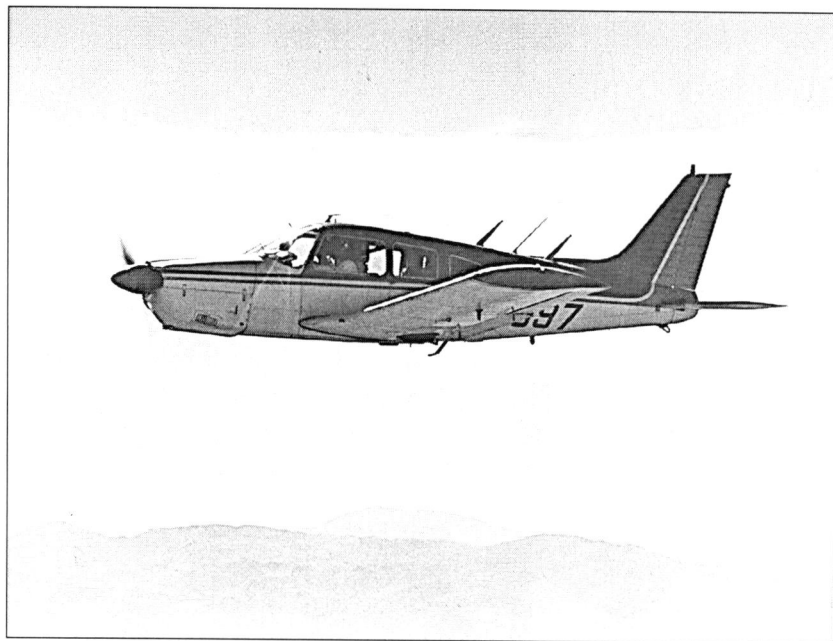

Arrow N41997 over Southern California

Chapter 7

Down the Strait

Airports are identified by the use of three letters (YVR for Vancouver) or a combination of letters and numbers for small airports (L05 for Siletz Bay). Like aircraft call signs, a prefix is added to identify the country: "C" for Canada and "K" for the United States. Canada's airplanes and airports both sport the C-prefix (seldom used, except outside Canada). United States airplanes carry an N-prefix, while airports have a "K" designator. Go figure.

In Canada, my first radio call to air traffic control always contains the "N." ATC usually foreshortens the call sign to the last three numbers – in my case, per air traffic control phonetics, "niner-niner-seven." Technically, a pilot cannot shorten the call sign to the last-three digits until ATC does so first.

When crossing the border back into the States, I'm careful to include the K-prefix for airports as I exit through Canadian airspace, although I doubt controllers are concerned. Bellingham is KBLI.

Bellingham has become an important airport for the Arrow. It's a convenient location to clear U.S. Customs and a personal stopping point on most trips to the States. In both Canada and the U.S., you only need to clear Customs upon arrival. You can depart from any airport on either side of the border, but only certain airports meet the criteria as a port of entry.

For many years, Port Angeles (KCLM) was my preferred point of entry to the United States, but the level of aviation activity there has diminished in recent years. Usually, the Customs agents have to come out to meet your airplane from the ferry terminal, and that sometimes leads to grumpy government employees. A good rule of thumb is to avoid grumpy Customs officials, at all costs. But Port Angeles is still a nice airport – there's something particularly attractive about descending over the Strait of Juan de Fuca on a clear day, with the glaciated Olympic Mountains dominating the horizon to the south.

When personal ties to Bellingham increase, KBLI replaces Port Angeles as my preferred port of entry. Margy's mom moves from California to Bellingham to be closer to us, and Arrow flights to KBLI become more frequent. It's now our first stop out of Canada and the final stop in the U.S. when returning from California.

* * * * *

Everyone seems to be in a good mood this morning. I make the required phone call to Bellingham Customs, and the agent's questions are minimal and his tone obliging. It's a good start.

The Nav Canada representative is similarly cheerful when I file my IFR flight plan by telephone. I'm used to filing flight plans by computer, but border-crossing flights into the States must be filed by phone. I fumble through the complicated (compared to U.S.) flight plan form, going down the list of required blocks of information. The cheery female voice accepts almost everything I provide, with only one minor interruption.

"Is that your time enroute?" she asks.

"Oh, no," I admit. "Five hours and zero minutes is my fuel on board. Time enroute is zero hours and fifty-five minutes." She knows Arrows are slow, but nothing is that slow.

An hour later, Margy and I are loading N41997 in Powell River, and it's the typical bag-drag. No matter how many times we cross the border, we always seem to load the airplane to its limit. Fortunately, it's hard to overload an Arrow with only two people aboard. Bodies are generally heavier than baggage (relative to their volume), but it's still wise to move the heavy items into the back seat and leave the baggage compartment for the lighter stuff. Our camping gear is always on board, so it doesn't take much more to fill the airplane.

On this trip to California, we're carrying a typical load. Aeronautical charts for Canada and the U.S. and numerous in-flight conveniences add to the cargo: snacks, water, satellite radio, reading material, jackets, survival kit, laptop computers, life vests (much of our flight is over water), and even a good-sized portable telescope. And then at least two luggage bags, for good measure. Almost everything we take goes round-trip, so the return flight will be no lighter.

The IFR departure procedure from Powell River is pretty standard. Margy takes care of the checklists and taxis to the ramp near the Flying Club's old (now deactivated) fuel pump. While she takes care of checking the airplane's subsystems (flight instruments, engine gauges, controls and switches), I take care of the ATC clearance.

I try contacting Comox Terminal on the radio, which sometimes works from the ground, but it pushes the communication range of our radios to their limit. On a bad day (in terms of radio atmospherics), I communicate with Comox by cell phone. Today is one of those bad days.

The Arrow's cabin is a noisy environment with the engine running, but the engine noise doesn't seem to bother the controller on the other end of the phone. On my end, it takes complete concentration to hear the controller's voice.

"November four-one-niner-niner-seven is cleared to the Bellingham Airport via Powell River, Alpha one-six, Active Pass, direct Bellingham. Climb and maintain five thousand. Squawk two-six-six-one. Comox Terminal is one-two-three decimal seven. Clearance void if not off by one-seven-four-zero. Will that give you enough time?"

It's a generous nine minutes, and we need less than five.

"That's plenty of time," I reply.

Then I read back the clearance and go back on intercom to discuss the details with Margy.

"Standard departure," I report. "Left turn out, climbing to five thousand. How's the airplane?"

"Everything's fine, but I held the run-up until you were finished with the phone."

The noisy run-up takes only a few seconds. Both magnetos check out fine, and the airflow over the cowl swooshes powerfully as Margy runs the prop lever through its full range. As she completes the checklist, I double-check the engine gauges. We're ready to go.

"Powell River Traffic, Arrow niner-niner-seven, back-taxiing on Runway Two-Seven for departure to the southeast, Powell River," I announce on the Unicom frequency.

At the end of the runway, Margy swings the airplane around and aligns it on the centerline. She pushes the throttle full forward, while holding the brakes with the tops of the rudder pedals.

"Doors and windows," she recites.

"Locked. I've got the transponder."

I make the brief departure announcement on Unicom frequency, flick the transponder to *ALT* (altitude encoding), and use the rotating knob to flip through the cylinder temperatures. All four cylinders register nearly the same in both cylinder head and exhaust gas temperatures – a good confirmation of proper engine performance at full power. Margy releases the brakes, and we begin to roll.

The airplane accelerates slowly in the thin, warm air. While Margy concentrates on the runway and the flight instruments, I watch the oil pressure gauge on her side of the cockpit, and cycle through CHT and EGT again. Takeoff is the most critical phase of flight, with the engine working the hardest.

We break ground smoothly. Margy raises the landing gear quickly to reduce drag but delays flap retraction until we are well clear of the power lines past the departure end of the runway. I like takeoffs on Runway 27. It's downhill, with a clear path out over the ocean.

After crossing Joyce Avenue, Margy turns left and climbs parallel to the shoreline. She retracts the flaps, one notch at a time, and then goes through her power reduction and climb checklist: throttle back to 25 inches of manifold pressure, prop 2500 rpm, fuel flow 12 gallons per hour, electric fuel pump off, strobe lights on. As she finishes the ritual, we pass abeam the ocean viewpoint parking area on Highway 101.

"Go for it," I say.

Margy uses both hands on the yoke to rotate the wheel firmly left, then right; then left and right again, and back to neutral. It's a wing-wag for Helen and Ed, watching our departure from their deck. And it means we are really leaving. In this case, it will be a full month in the States, not a particularly pleasant thought. It's fortunate that flying is so much fun, or you'd never get me to leave.

* * * * *

The amber route (Alpha 16) takes us across Texada Island to MACAR Intersection, mid-channel in the Strait of Georgia. We're on a non-directional beacon route, unheard of in the States for over four decades. Today's flight will take us over Nanaimo; then a left turn (more NDB navigation) to Active Pass in the Gulf Islands north of Victoria.

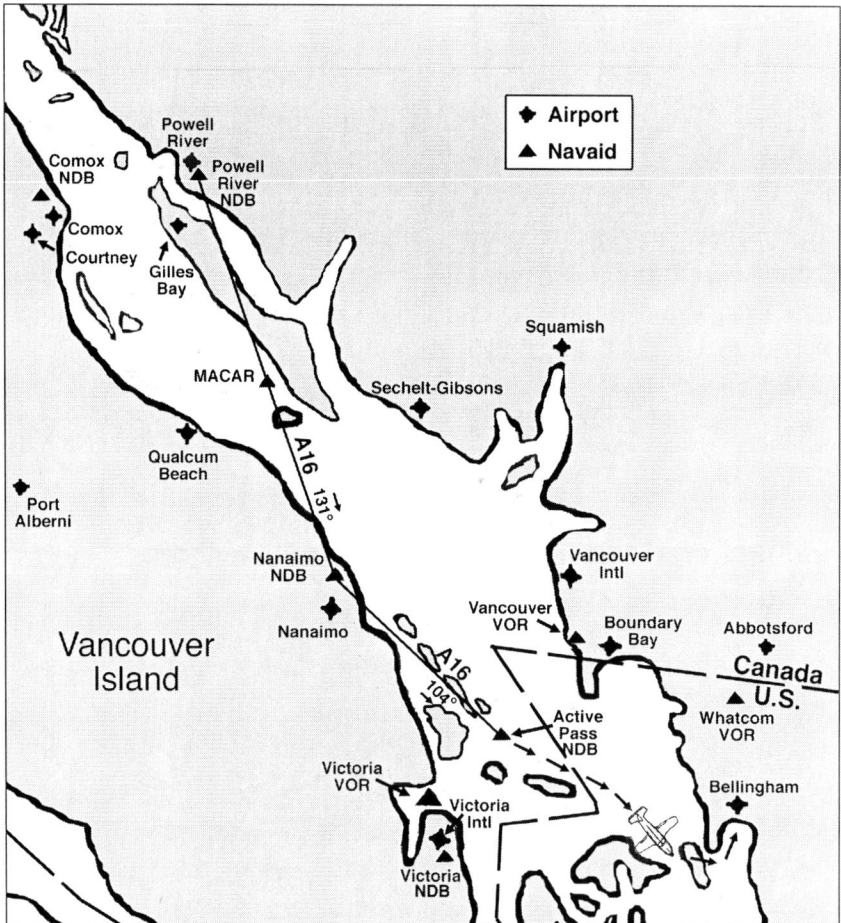

Of course, I cheat a bit. The GPS receiver is set to a waypoint, a "phantom station" that coincides with Nanaimo NDB. I'm tracking to the waypoint, using my user-friendly horizontal situation indicator (HSI). It's more accurate than using the old-fashioned NDB receiver, called the ADF (automatic direction finder). But I back up the GPS with the signal from the NDB. When using a VFR-only GPS, that makes things legal.

It's clear today, so I cheat even more. I reset the ADF to the Powell River AM station, turn up the volume, and listen to the news and weather for a few minutes, which means I'm not using the ADF to track the signal to Nanaimo. But I closely monitor our track with the GPS, while visually checking our progress across the strait, so it's plenty safe. When I see Nanaimo's harbour growing larger over the Arrow's nose, I reset the ADF to the NDB to confirm station passage, and stand by for the required 30-degree heading change to the left.

Margy makes the turn and continues along A16 towards Active Pass, still navigating with the GPS, backed up by the ADF. It's a beautiful route along the southern coast of Vancouver Island, directly over the Gulf Islands.

"Dodd Narrows is really rippin'," says Margy.

White water is streaming northward through the constricted channel. A small boat is plowing into the narrows.

From the air, the Gulf Islands spread out along the edge of Vancouver Island, all the way to Victoria. I've kayaked many of these islands, and the view from down there is even more sublime. Being on the water is both absorbing and demanding. From above, traveling at twice highway speed, it's all too easy. From the cockpit of the Arrow, these beautiful islands are reduced to a quick traverse that consumes less than a half hour, seeming to diminish their prominence. Still, it's a pretty sight from up here.

By now, things have settled down enough for me to start setting up a maze of wires for the long flight to California. First comes the yoke-mounted GPS. The small black box is not tied into the aircraft's avionics display, but in many ways it's better than a panel-mounted satellite receiver. The small electronic moving map keeps me oriented, the miniature airplane symbol tracking towards labeled islands and aeronautical checkpoints. From my side of the cockpit (the right side), it gives me interesting data to monitor. I fly comfortably from this seat, so much so that it is my preferred location even when flying solo. I'm a menace to myself in the left seat, always feeling uncomfortable with left fingers on the yoke and reaching for the throttle with my right hand.

The portable GPS requires an antenna on the glare shield and a cord in the DC power receptacle. From my seat, I'm in charge of the relatively bare right side of the panel: two GPS receivers, the VORs, and the defroster lever (which I refer to as the "flight instructor's control"). Margy takes care of almost everything else from the left seat. Of course, I can talk to ATC, and that's my favorite duty. I leave most of the takeoffs to Margy, and hog a few of the landings, but I'm fully content with my primary duties – communicating with ATC and in charge of navigation.

After the portable GPS finds its satellites, I begin setting up more equipment and another batch of wires. This time it's the satellite radio for music and news. I'm speaking here of XM satellite radio, a wonderful in-flight luxury. Tuning AM radio stations with the ADF gets old fast. Stations drift quickly out of range. Besides, AM is more talk shows and advertisements than music. But with the satellite radio, I can listen to news and music all the way to California. Of course, it too requires a dashboard antenna and a DC power cord. So now I must hook up a DC splitter. As you can imagine, getting in and out of the airplane through my spaghetti of wires is a challenge in itself.

As the Gulf Islands slip below us, controllers at Victoria Terminal vector us towards Bellingham, in preparation for the visual approach. Runway 34 is in use, so a left turn will line us up with the final approach path. Snow-capped Mount Baker appears directly off our nose, dominating the eastern horizon like a geographic locator beacon.

We report to ATC that the airport is in sight, and Victoria issues their final Canadian instructions: "Niner-niner-seven is cleared for the visual approach. Contact Bellingham Tower, one-two-four decimal nine."

It's the last "decimal" frequency I'll be issued for a month. In the States, everything is "point" this and "point" that, a minor variation, but enough to remind me that Canada ATC phraseology is unique.

The control tower asks us to report three miles west for a left base leg to Runway 34. Margy sets up a gradual descent, and we glide effortlessly towards the airport. Some days you don't even have to touch the power. You just continue downward at a steady pace, while making minor adjustments in pitch trim for the changes in drag. This is one of those days.

I make the three-mile report. Margy lowers the landing gear, then the first notch of flaps, flicking the trim switch on her yoke to compensate for changes in pitch.

"Three green," she reports.

I glance at the landing gear lights to verify her call-out. As the saying goes: there are only two types of pilots who fly retractable gear airplanes – those who have landed gear up, and those who will. Margy and I double-check the gear lights repeatedly on every landing.

We pass over the harbour, Margy maneuvering to line up with Runway 34 and adding another notch of flaps. Then she pulls back slightly on the wheel to set up an airspeed of 90 MPH, immediately resetting the pitch trim to relieve the yoke backpressure. We slip in over the cliffs near the approach end of the runway.

"Three green, prop forward, landing checklist complete," she says aloud, more for herself than for me.

"Niner-niner-seven, cleared to land, Runway Three-Four," announces the tower.

It's a good landing, main gear first, with the nose held high until it falls from its own weight.

Fifty-five minutes, point-to-point. Now, that's efficiency.

"We'd like to taxi to Customs," I tell the ground controller.

"Cleared to Customs," he confirms. "Are you familiar?"

Familiar? Yes, we're familiar. In fact, it's beginning to seem like home.

* * * * *

By 2007, Margy and I are spending more time stateside in Bellingham than in Los Angeles. Flights to California in the Arrow are comfortable from May to October, but don't try to plan anything that relies on a fixed schedule during the rest of the year. Flying in the Pacific Northwest in a small airplane is a major challenge from late autumn until early spring, due to extreme weather systems. Time to spare, go by air.

We settle into Bellingham as our stateside residence, although we still need to make occasional trips back to Los Angeles for business and to seek some warm winter sun.

With KBLI as our primary U.S. destination, we now have an opportunity to leisurely explore the region by air. One of the priority destinations is Skagit Regional Airport, just south of Bellingham. Margy and I visit the airport by car one day, in an attempt to locate the "twin" to our Arrow. Originally, this airplane was the production Arrow featured in 1975 magazine advertisements for Piper Aircraft. Our friend, David, who possesses an uncanny ability to remember the tail number of any aircraft he has ever flown (a lot of airplanes) or even seen (a whole lot more), has sent us on this chase.

David found the 1975 *Flying* magazine advertisement in his prodigious collection of old periodicals, and presented it to me without comment. I scanned the full-page ad for several minutes before I realized his point – this tail number was only one digit different from our cherished N41997, a 1974 Piper Arrow. But David won't let it rest at that. He investigates the registration history of N41998 on the Internet and discovers that the tail number was recently relicensed to an aircraft owner with records that indicate "Bow, Washington," only a few miles from Skagit Regional Airport.

Margy and I drive our car around the airport's perimeter, trying to find the N-number. Since September 11, 2001, aviation is a different world, and most small airports are securely fenced, with limited access. From the automobile parking lot, we are able to view only a few aircraft, and most are too distant to read the numbers on their fuselages. It would be much easier to investigate from the other side of the fence. So one sunny day, we fly to Skagit Regional Airport.

We slip into the traffic pattern on a Friday afternoon, when the activity level is amazingly high. After our visit by car, we are unsure why this airport is so large in the first place. It sits near Edison and Bow, tiny Washington communities. Even with larger cities nearby (Burlington and Mount Vernon), the combined population doesn't seem large enough to support this major airport. Two runways (one 5500 feet long), a corporate jet center, and new roads entering the airfield make Skagit Regional seem like a large commercial airport in the middle of nowhere. What could support such a costly infrastructure?

The answer, as evidenced by the congested Unicom frequency that serves the airport, is flight training. As we approach from the north, a Cessna 172 reports downwind, simulating an engine failure and forced landing. Another Cessna is approaching from the south and hears our report, as we begin our descent.

"Piper north of Skagit, please say again your position and altitude," requests the pilot.

"Arrow niner-niner-seven is three north, descending through two thousand five hundred," I reply. "We're planning left traffic for Runway Two-Eight."

"Okay, you'll be ahead of me. I'll be looking."

He's looking, and so are we; and we're also listening carefully on the common traffic advisory frequency (CTAF), as several other aircraft report various stages of takeoff and landing. Still, other airplanes may be in the traffic pattern without radios, since none are required here. It reminds me of Corona Airport in southern California, a small airport full of training aircraft without radios. I avoid Corona like the plague.

As I try to space the Arrow on the 45-degree entry for the downwind leg, Margy is snapping photos.

"Hey, give me a hand with the traffic," I say.

It's more of an admonition than a request. This place is unpleasantly busy. Separation of aircraft is monitored visually, pilot-to-pilot, coupled with careful listening on the radio for pilot reports issued in-the-blind, a phrase that pretty well describes its value in a situation like this. Such a system works fine when there is little traffic, but not today. Margy immediately puts her camera away and helps me scan for renegade aircraft.

I cut the base leg short, trying to get on the ground and out of the way as quickly as possible. Once clear of the runway, I relax a bit and taxi towards a ramp that is full of aircraft. Even during taxiing, aircraft zip back and forth, every which way, like a field full of anxious squirrels. As I taxi between two rows of airplanes, I come nose to nose with a Cessna 182. We slip out through an empty space between two parked planes, onto another taxiway.

"You keep a lookout for Nine-Nine-Eight, while I try to keep us from getting whacked," I say.

Margy examines the N-numbers as we weave our way down the ramp. We realize that many aircraft are out of sight inside hangars, but it's still worth a try. At the end of the parking area, we reverse course and taxi back to Runway Two-Eight on the less-congested parallel taxiway, without success in locating our Arrow's twin. A few minutes later, we are airborne, glad to leave this crowded airport behind.

* * * * *

One of my favorite destinations in the Bellingham area is Port Townsend's Jefferson County Airport. The first time Margy and I land there, it is to visit Gary and Linda, our friends from nearby Sequim (pronounced "Squim"). The airport is a pleasant surprise.

We navigate southbound from Bellingham, alongside Whidbey Island. The ATC radar facility at Whidbey Naval Air Station ("approach control") handles our Arrow efficiently, keeping us out of the complex of military operating areas (MOAs) and rings of Class C airspace. Margy flies while I navigate.

As we pass abeam the military runway, a departing two-engine S-3 Viking reports an engine failure to Whidbey Approach, declaring an emergency and requesting an immediate return to Whidbey. We listen as the air traffic controller handles the situation calmly and efficiently.

The pilot speaks like Chuck Yeager, never breaking his inflection, as if this happens every day. In a few minutes, the S-3 is handed off to the control tower, and approach control returns to its usual broadcasts of aircraft checking in and requesting traffic advisories.

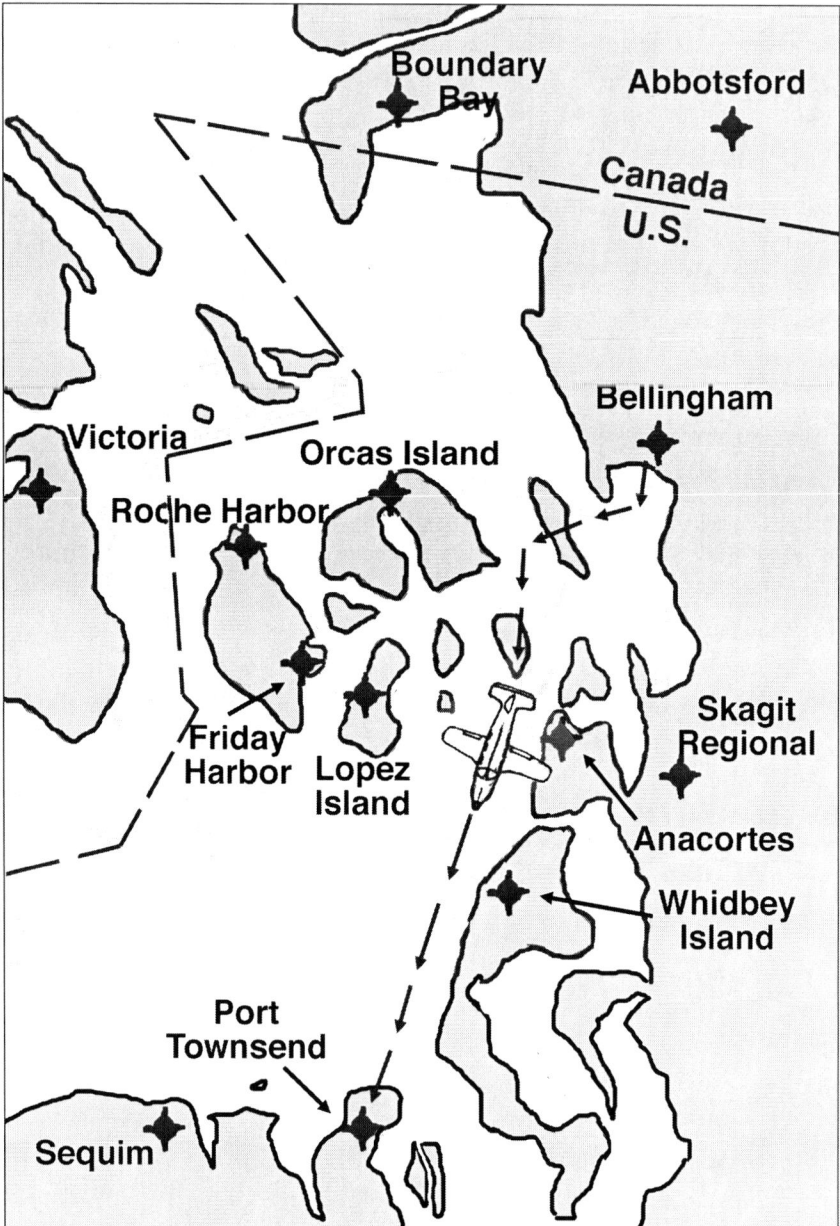

Port Townsend's 3000-foot runway needs to be handled with care in our Arrow. But the clear zones are spacious, and operations are comfortable with today's partial fuel load and minimal baggage.

Immediately after landing, we are treated to an airport environment reminiscent of pre-2001. There is no airport fence, a rarity these days even at small airports without airline activity. One-way taxiways in and out, a bustling airport cafe, and abundant transient parking adds to the comfortable atmosphere.

Gary drives us to town, stopping along the way to show us the local boat repair yard. What an unexpected facility it is! Huge wheeled cradles bring boats up from the docks to the work yard, reminding me of the giant crawlers that haul the space shuttle to its launch pad. We walk around the shipyard, inspecting boats in all stages of marine maintenance.

A sailboat, the same model as Gary and Linda's 35-foot Island Packet, sits on blocks, allowing us to closely examine the design from the bottom up. The boat's unique full-length steel keel amazes me, as does the opportunity to see close up the inboard engine's drive shaft, prop, and rudder.

After spending a leisurely day in town (and a typically expensive visit to the West Marine boat shop – we buy two pair of binoculars), Gary drives us back to the airport. Even with a stiff headwind to reduce our roll, Margy and I agree that I should make the takeoff. Margy normally performs this duty, and she does it well. But today we both feel a bit uncomfortable with the shorter runway length, particularly because we will be taking off on Runway 27, which has a smaller departure clear zone. Two-Seven is the wise choice with today's prevailing wind, but it's still a bit daunting.

The Arrow gets off the ground quickly in the headwind, and I retract the landing gear immediately to get us up and away efficiently. The climb is comfortable, with a left turn to join the downwind leg, then up and over the airport to head northbound towards Bellingham. I'm concentrating on the departure, with little attention to the radio, but I hear a pilot reporting on the common traffic advisory frequency at another airport.

"That sounds like Tyrone," says Margy.

"You're right, it does. How can that be?"

"I swear he reported in the pattern at Powell River, and I think the call sign was E-T-L."

ETL is the Westview Flying Club's Cessna 172. I glance at the communication radio, set to 123.0 Megahertz. The Unicom frequency for Port Townsend is the same as Powell River. We are listening to our friend, Tyrone, talking on his radio in the traffic pattern at Powell River! Port Townsend is 130 kilometres south of the border, and Powell River is over 200 kilometres line-of-sight from here. Perceptually, the separation between us is even farther.

Radio transmissions can be received over 200 kilometres on a good day, when both aircraft are well above the horizon, but still it surprises us. It gives us a warm feeling to hear Tyrone all the way down here in Port Townsend, making us feel that much closer to our self-proclaimed home airport in another country.

◊ ◊ ◊ ◊ ◊ ◊ ◊

Chapter 8

More Unexpected Destinations

A unique sense of adventure accompanies unexpected destinations. In small aircraft, such locations are usually visited because of weather or mechanical problems. Sometimes the places you land are unplanned for other reasons.

Most of my flying in Canadian airspace has been in the western provinces, since my home base is California. Just getting to British Columbia is an 1800-kilometre flight. One summer, however, I find an opportunity to explore Quebec. A young flight student of mine, Carl, is getting married near Buffalo, New York, at the same time that I plan to visit relatives in central New York State. This trip will provide an opportunity to experience two of my favorite activities: camping and flying. Carl and I devise a plan. I will miss Carl's wedding, but I'll make up for it by going with him on his honeymoon.

Margy and I meet Carl and Laurie at Syracuse Airport. Carl brings a rental Cessna 172 from Buffalo. Since we've travelled to New York by airline, Margy and I rent a Piper Warrior at Syracuse. Our plan is to travel north, staying the first night at Mont-Laurier, Quebec, and then continue on farther north into more remote regions, to the town of Chibougamau. From there, we will travel east and then south to Bar Harbor, Maine, and finally back to Syracuse. It's an itinerary that inspires our adventurous spirit. Carl is a 100-hour private pilot who normally would not attempt such a challenging trip. He looks up to me as a seasoned Canadian pilot, although I've never flown in the eastern provinces (nor am I Canadian).

One of our primary challenges involves packing in California for a camping trip involving rental aircraft. We need to condense our luggage for our airline travel to New York. Besides camping equipment, we will require supplies for our rental aircraft. Neither of us has charts for the proposed route, so that is one item that doesn't need to be packed. I assume it will be easy to obtain the necessary charts in New York. What I don't know is that New York State might as well be 1000 kilometres from Canada. No Canadian charts are available in Syracuse, but they should be plentiful once we arrive in Canada. The New York sectional chart and its associated World Aeronautical Chart (WAC) take us across the border and into Mont-Laurier. From there we can count on getting new Canadian charts. It is a reasonable plan, but only in theory.

We arrive in Canada late in the afternoon, just in time to avoid Customs overtime charges at Smith Falls, Ontario. By the time our entry paperwork is complete, it's already getting late. So we quickly get airborne, over-fly Ottawa, and head for our planned fuel stop at Maniwaki, Quebec. The gas pumps are still open when we arrive, but all else is closed.

My sure-thing stop to purchase charts that include Chibougamau is a bust, but there's still plenty of daylight left on this high-latitude, summer evening. Before departing for our planned overnight camping spot (Mont-Laurier), a local pilot comes to our rescue. He has extra copies of the regional charts, and is pleased to share them with us. Of course, these charts are several editions old, but important information seldom changes on VFR charts from one publication cycle to the next. Famous last words.

We make it into Mont-Laurier well before dark, early enough for a swim at the small lake near the airport. But before we enter the water, a very excited young man runs towards us, waving his arms and yelling: "Billet, billet!" He points to a nearby sign that displays French words apparently explaining that it costs money to swim here. This is our first reminder that this is the French speaking part of Canada, and we'd better get used to it. We pay our money, and go for a swim.

We plan to depart at the crack of dawn, before the summer convection works itself into uncomfortable turbulence. So that evening, Carl and I pour over the charts, preparing as thoroughly as possible for the next leg of the trip.

In our previous flying, we've both planned routes with detailed dead reckoning calculations, but this is the first time either of us has flown extensively without ground-based navigational aids. Neither of our rental aircraft have LORAN nor GPS, and no VOR or NDB stations are aligned with our route. This will be a major challenge, requiring basic dead reckoning – raw calculations of enroute time, speed, and distance. Our lack of reliable data involving winds aloft for this region will increase the importance of precise identification of visual landmarks – a critical navigational backup. The chart shows few usable checkpoints, except for the occasional remote road and hundreds (seemingly thousands!) of small lakes.

* * * * *

The next morning we are airborne right after dawn, flying in clear skies with small puffy cumulus clouds already growing to the north. We have minimal weather information for our route, but the general forecast indicates that conditions will be good, though not perfect. As the day warms, we expect increasing turbulence from routine convection. Our gas tanks are full, and that means we will have plenty of fuel to get to Chibougamau, but we'd better not miss our destination. There are no charted alternate airports within the range of our airplanes. For the first time ever, we need to compute our point-of-no-return, the spot along our route where we cannot turn back to Mount-Laurier, considering our fuel reserves. At that magical point, we will be committed to locating Chibougamau.

We settle into a loose formation, remaining within visual range of each other. Carl leads, since he has the least experience, and that is the easiest position to fly in a relaxed cross-country formation. From behind, Margy and I navigate, calling out heading changes to Carl over the radio as ground checkpoints appear. Our flight progress indicates that the winds aloft are pushing us slightly off course, but we correct our headings quickly. Margy identifies landmarks along the way, comparing them to the chart detail. She confirms our location primarily by the shape of the numerous lakes below us. This is an area of expertise for her, so we swap our normal flight assignments. She navigates while I fly, with Carl always in sight in front of us.

After the first hour, it gets a little bumpy, an indication of what lies ahead. The clouds are building quickly, with a few towering cumulus scattered among the fair weather puffs of white against a stunning blue sky. We pass our computed point-of-no-return, the mathematical spot where we are committed to reaching our destination. There is no longer adequate fuel to return to our point of departure. The constant radio chatter between our airplanes has a calming effect. So far, there are no significant problems, but the developing weather patterns could get interesting.

"Margy has confirmed our position at the point-of-no-return," I report to Carl over the radio. "Right on course, with no heading change necessary."

"Roger," replies Carl. "All is well here."

I visualize Laurie holding on for dear life. She is young, married only a few days, and not particularly comfortable in small airplanes. Here we are, flying over a remote section of Canada, entering convective conditions and bouncing around a bit. Hopefully, Carl has explained to Laurie the meaning of point-of-no-return with the loving gentleness of a new husband.

The previous night, we camped next to our airplanes, something new in Laurie's realm of experience. It was a beautiful, warm evening, but the black flies were out in force. In the morning, Laurie's forehead was a mass of welts. Her bridal hair-do provided a particular chemical attraction for the flies. Marital bliss – flying in a small Cessna over remote Quebec, weather deteriorating, getting bumpy, itchy forehead, point-of-no-return, and a new husband-pilot with only 100 hours of flight experience. What could be better? The answer comes to me in Carl's next radio call.

"It's starting to hail!" Carl yells over the radio. "It's battering the hell out of us!"

My first reaction is this must be Carl's idea of a joke. These are mostly fair weather clouds, with a few towering cumulus off to the sides. It takes a full-blown thunderstorm to spew out hail. I can see Carl about a kilometre in front of us, now under a fair-sized cumulus cloud with what looks like a rain shower slanting downward. If it's really hail, this is a serious encounter for a small Cessna and a novice pilot.

"Carl, I have you clearly in sight. You're under a small cumulus cloud and maybe in a rain shower. But it can't be hail."

I try to sound confident. But my attention is riveted on the situation. I've led a novice pilot into remote territory, and now he's in trouble!

"It's hail, I'm pretty sure," replies Carl, a bit calmer now. "It's pelting the heck out of us."

Then it dawns on me. Carl learned to fly in sunny southern California. It's possible that none of his 100 hours of flying have been in anything except near-perfect conditions.

"Okay, Carl. I understand. But have you ever flown in rain before?"

"No," states Carl curtly. "But this isn't rain. It's hail!"

"It's rain. I'm sure of it," I reply, finally understanding Carl's situation. "It sounds like hail on that thin plexiglass windshield."

The first time you enter rain in a small airplane, it gets your attention. The impact of drops on the thin windshield, along with the "tin can" structure of the airframe, raises a major clamor inside the cockpit.

When you're flying over remote terrain, as a new pilot, it must sound even worse.

"Okay," radios Carl, his voice under control again. "I think you're right, it's only rain."

Now that the crisis is over, we all get a good laugh. With our first major obstacle so quickly behind us, we are more relaxed. But I'm not sure about Laurie. Since I can't talk to her on the radio, it's my guess she is now beyond the white-knuckle stage.

* * * * *

As we cross our last critical checkpoint, a dirt road along a series of small lakes, Margy confirms that we are still on course. Chibougamau is now only 50 miles ahead. This is a good location for the Cessna and Warrior to exchange positions.

"How about throttling back a little, while maintaining your altitude," I radio to Carl. "I'll pass on your left and lead us down into the traffic pattern."

We exchange positions, and Carl falls into a loose formation behind me, a few kilometres back to give him easy maneuvering room. For now, we'll maintain our altitude until the airport is in sight. Then we'll begin our descent into the traffic pattern. I don't expect much traffic, but we'll enter the pattern together. I'll absorb the burden of the radio communications, reporting our arrival as a "flight of two." For a new pilot like Carl, landing at an airport he has never seen before will be enough of a challenge.

About seven miles out, we identify the runway, and Margy and I simultaneously notice the same amazing predicament.

"Do you see what I see?" she asks. Her voice registers disbelief.

"I think so," I reply. "It looks like huge mounds of dirt on the runway."

We marvel at the sight – a long paved runway with gigantic piles of dirt spaced every few hundred feet down the centerline. This single-runway airport is closed, for sure, and probably has been for some time. Those free charts from the Mont-Laurier pilot must be plenty old.

"Can't be," says Margy. "They couldn't just close a major airport like this."

As Margy speaks on the intercom, I hear Carl's voice on the radio in the background. He's right behind us, and in just a few moments he's going to see the same thing we see.

"Do you have the airport in sight yet," he asks innocently.

New pilot, remote territory, hailstorm, new wife, and a closed runway. The nearest alternate airport is now beyond our fuel range. This is not going to be easy to explain.

"Yes, we have the runway, right in front of us," I reply. It isn't a lie.

"Shall we begin our descent?" asks Carl.

"Not yet – there's a little problem."

Little problem, indeed. We talk over the situation, four reasonably intelligent people, but no good ideas. I'm in charge, so I make a decision for the sake of making a decision.

"Tune in the NDB to our northwest, frequency two-four-five, and let's start towards it," I suggest.

It's not much of a plan, but I figure we should head towards a known location. Maybe we can find an uncharted field near the NDB. There's really no reason that should be true, but it sets us into a course of action while we reorganize. We still have over an hour of fuel left.

The local Flight Service frequency is already tuned in my second radio. When I turn up the volume, it's a clutter of French-speaking pilots – not a single English voice on the channel. English is the international standard of air traffic control. Apparently, no one bothered telling this to pilots in Quebec. I've heard that radio communications in this province are more often conducted in French than you'll find when flying in France. I believe it.

I broadcast our situation in-the-blind, hoping a nearby pilot will hear the call and answer in English. It's not an emergency (yet), but I'm sure my tone indicates the level of stress I feel.

A Beaver on floats immediately answers my transmission.

"Warrior seven-three-charlie, this is DeHavilland foxtrot-delta-tango. I read you loud and clear."

It's a voice out of heaven, and I breathe a sigh of relief.

"We're just north of Chibougamau airport," I reply immediately. "The runway appears to be closed. Would you be familiar with the nearest usable airport relative to our position?"

"You must be at the old Chibougamau airfield," the fluent English-speaker replies. "They've moved the airport to the NDB, so just continue northwest a few miles, and you'll see it."

Oh.

In a few minutes, the airport appears off our nose. We enter the traffic pattern in formation and land without further incident. We park near two large twin-engine amphibians, water-scooping aircraft on standby, ready to be deployed to fight forest fires. This is a common sight at Canadian airports during the summer. Our tiny Cessna and Piper look like two small children nestled under the protective wings of their elders. I sit in my airplane, engine off, finally winding down after the "excitement" of finding a closed runway.

At the car rental counter in the small terminal, I realize I have repeatedly pronounced Chibougamau on the Flight Service frequency just the way it is spelled (Chi-bow-ga-maw). That must have resulted in a lot of laughs from French-speaking pilots listening to my radio transmissions. It's actually pronounced Chi-boo-gah-moo.

Lesson: Don't use outdated charts. And, unless you speak French, watch out when flying in remote areas of Quebec.

* * * * *

Another trip in the eastern provinces leads to a stop for fuel and an overnight camping site that seems ideal, at first glance.

The minute I hear its name, Big Trout Lake becomes an obvious camping destination. At the Flight Service Station in Thompson, Manitoba, I discuss fuel availability at airports leading to Moosonee, Ontario (adjacent to Moose Factory Island), our destination on James Bay. To view this famous place (at the lower end of Hudson Bay) from the air is an exciting prospect. Now we are within one fuel stop of achieving that goal.

Forest fires blanket northern Ontario, but Big Trout Lake is an airport located almost directly on the path to Moosonee, and should be easy to locate. The current weather report shows Big Trout exceeding VFR minimums, but with smoke in all quadrants. Although we are capable of IFR, the only instrument approach into Big Trout will be via non-directional beacon. They don't call NDB arrivals "non-precision approaches" for nothing.

The Flight Service specialist verifies that Big Trout has fuel, and the weather between here and there looks good. If the visibility is unacceptable along the way because of the smoke, we have plenty of fuel to turn around and come back.

The flight turns out pleasantly uneventful. Approaching Big Trout Lake, visibility deteriorates rapidly, but we sneak in through the smoke without a problem. It's an airport that lives up to its name. I'm not sure about the trout (no fishing pole aboard), but the lake is within walking distance, and so is the First Nations village.

We carry enough gas to make it to Moosonee without additional fuel, but it never hurts to top-off when gas is available, especially in remote areas. We can take on an additional 60 litres at Big Trout, if we can find someone to pump it. We park next to the fuel hose, but a sign on the shed announces: "Fuel Attendant in Town." It must not be a very big town.

Margy and I walk down the road to the tiny village, stopping for a 7-Up at a house that advertises *Hot Dogs and Drinks Here*. It's a refreshing stop on a warm July day.

The first commercial shop we come to is the office of the local airline, with a sign outside that says: *Bearskin Lake Air Service*. The airline's Twin Otters are the only realistic way to get in and out of Big Trout Lake, so it's a small but booming business. A barely-English-speaking gas attendant gives us a ride back to the airport to refuel the Arrow.

It's difficult to communicate with the young attendant, so I use hand signals to explain the simple situation – to the top with the fuel. After pumping 58 litres, the young man struggles with paper and pen, trying to multiply the quantity of gas by the price per litre. I offer to help, but he shrugs me away. Since I don't know the fuel price, I can't assist. It saddens me to watch him try to multiply these numbers. Is this a disadvantage he will have to live with forever?

After a few more minutes, the young man digs an electronic calculator out of the shed and tries again. This time he comes up with a number: $185!

This was only a top-off, less than 60 litres. I quickly do the mental math – over $3 per litre. Surely there is an error. We'll need to return to town to pay our fuel bill, so we'll resolve it there.

There is no error. The cashier explains the situation – all fuel has to be flown in to this airport at great expense. "Bladder birds" (Twin Otters with internal rubber tanks full of fuel) bring the gas in during the night.

The bladder birds make a noisy addition to our overnight experience near the end of the runway. Our camping spot is in the dirt, but comfortable, except for the thunder of the twin-engine airplanes coming and going all night long.

Lesson: When you ask Flight Service about fuel availability, you might also inquire about the price. And don't camp near a busy gas station.

* * * * *

The next morning, we're up early and ready to depart for Moosonee. The smoke is thicker today, but the forecast is for improving conditions as we fly eastward. The takeoff is conducted using instrument flight rules, but with the unusual condition of having no communication with air traffic control, no clearance, and no flight plan. This is uncontrolled airspace (Class G), so a flight plan would be meaningless. We are outside ATC's area of jurisdiction, so we simply climb aboard, select an appropriate IFR route and altitude, and go. It's a strange feeling, but perfectly legal, though we are flying in near zero visibility with no one to talk to.

The route I select is from Big Trout NDB direct to Moosonee NDB. By my computation, an outbound bearing from Big Trout should link nicely with the inbound bearing to Moosonee. I expect a few miles of dead reckoning between the stations, too far from either NDB for an adequate signal. The terrain is flat, and traffic is minimal. I've flown in conditions with much higher risk. Nevertheless, it's an unsettling feeling to be flying in minimal visibility with no air traffic control to guide you on your way.

All goes well. The smoke is disconcerting, but I expect it to disperse as we leave the fire area. The air is smooth, but it's awfully quiet without the normal backdrop of ATC communications. As we draw away from Big Trout, the NDB signal dwindles to nothing. So I pick a heading that has worked so far, and press on between the beacons, hoping the winds aloft have not changed.

Partly to have someone to talk to and partly to update the wind data, I try contacting Arctic Radio. After several tries, I'm answered by an Air Canada flight that hears my calls and offers to relay my message to the Flight Service Station. In this remote country, the big guys look out for the little guys. Of course, the big guys used to be little guys themselves.

The winds aloft, relayed by Air Canada, are close to what I have expected. So I maintain my current heading and await the next NDB signal. In another fifteen minutes, nearly two full hours after departing Big Trout, the ADF needle starts to home on Moosonee. Almost immediately, we fly out of the smoke into clear skies.

The land below us is flat in all directions. On the horizon ahead, I get my first glimpse of Hudson Bay, an awesome moment. Actually, it's James Bay, the lower extension of Hudson Bay. But it's all connected, and finally I am here.

The Arrow pushes past Moose Factory Island and out over James Bay, before looping back for landing. The water below may look like any other large body of water, but this is a personal achievement. It's a private moment of celebration, never to be experienced in the same way again. We cruise in the smooth air over James Bay, celebrating the great Canadian north. Then I swing the Arrow around and point the nose towards the modern paved runway at Moosonee.

◊ ◊ ◊ ◊ ◊ ◊ ◊

Chapter 9

CYPW and the South Coast

Although it is easy to learn Canadian flight regulations without knowing anything about Canadian pilots, getting a feel for differences in pilot communities is a good way to understand local flight procedures. Joining the Westview Flying Club in Powell River gave me insight into the character of pilots in British Columbia. Not surprisingly, they are similar to pilots in the States – intelligent, innovative individuals who realistically balance risk and reward. Also not unexpected, they love the aviation environment and pursue it as a process of lifelong learning. CYPW (Powell River) becomes an airport that teaches me a lot about Canadian aviators.

Don, one of the quiet characters at our club meetings, has pursued every opportunity to fly a wide variety of aircraft. If someone lands at the Powell River Airport in a make or model Don has not yet flown, he is ready to barter for a chance to fly it. Photos of Don's "flight line" adorn one wall of the clubhouse. In 53 years of flying (as of 2008), he has flown 51 different makes and models of aircraft, and still counting.

Dale, another flying club member, is one of the guys whose advice I consider gospel truth, especially after an incident involving an engine noise he heard when I flew overhead.

"I heard you coming home yesterday," he said. "You flew right over my house. Your engine sounds louder than normal."

"Loud? What do you mean?"

"Oh, I don't know. It just sounded throatier than a fuel injected Lycoming usually sounds."

An engine is an engine. Surely the sound of an engine from 3000 feet isn't perceptively different from one day to the next. Yet, this is Dale talking, so I'm attentive to what he is saying.

"My engine is running fine. I haven't noticed any changes recently."

"Probably nothing, but it still sounds unusually throaty."

Coming from Dale, I wonder what this means. Dale isn't a licensed aircraft mechanic, but he is a wizard with absolutely anything mechanical. Although I do nothing about his comments except to wonder what they mean, I soon wish I had been more proactive. Two weeks later, my engine suffers from a broken oil control ring, an occurrence almost unheard of in Lycoming engines.

I listen to Dale's flying stories with just a touch of suspicion. Surely he couldn't have experienced as many mechanical failures, weather incidents, and run-ins with air traffic control as it sounds. But when I meet Dale's wife, his reluctant passenger, I realize he has understated his aerial antics. After taking an early retirement from the paper mill, he flew as an independent contractor for a local charter company, hauling passengers to BC destinations in a Piper 235 (Dakota) and a Cherokee Six. The challenges of local geography and weather, coupled with Dale's natural affinity for in-flight adventures, undoubtedly resulted in an occasional incredulous passenger.

Don and Dale are accomplished pilots, but Wally tops the list. Pilots like Wally have been-there and done-that in an amazing variety of situations. In Wally's case, most of that experience has been logged in a floatplane on wilderness waterways along the BC coast.

Wally began his flying career in airplanes on wheels, and was later endorsed to fly floats by his mentor, a commercial floatplane pilot. At the time, this was the most common route to becoming licensed on floats. Wally first trained in a Cessna 140 (on wheels) at Vancouver Airport (now Vancouver International), where he hung out as a kid, working on airplanes for free.

He remembers the arrival of the first trans-Pacific flight from Australia in the late 1940s. Wally heard the four-engine DC-4 fly overhead on a foggy morning, making several low passes in an attempt to land. Finally, the aircraft broke out of the clouds for just a few seconds, off to the side of the runway.

"The pilot must have thought he'd seen enough," relates Wally. "So he cranked 'er over like a fighter and put 'er on the runway, just like that."

When Wally was flying his Cessna trainer in the early 1950s, he'd takeoff and land on a grass triangle beyond the paved runway used by the airliners. Light signals from the control tower provided his traffic pattern instructions.

"Green cleared you across the paved runway for takeoff on the grass. And if you were a bad boy, you'd get a white light, which meant you should report to the tower – you're gonna get whipped."

Radio requirements applied only to the airliners, but were gradually phased in for training aircraft. At first, Wally used the radio for taxi and takeoff only, while landings were still controlled by light signals. Since military aircraft were also assigned to Vancouver, it was a busy mix of aircraft. Wally recalls one day when he was cleared to cross the paved runway by radio, but took a moment to double-check for traffic before advancing the throttle. A voice from the control tower hollered: "Get crackin'!" – as a flight of four P-51 Mustangs in formation bore down on him on their final approach. Wally punched the throttle forward and crossed the runway, thus avoiding the dreaded "invitation" to the tower.

After obtaining his private license, Wally transitioned from wheeled airplanes to floatplanes. By then, he had moved to Powell River, joined the Powell River Flying Club (later the Westview Flying Club), and purchased a Luscombe floatplane. His initial checkout in the Luscombe was on Powell Lake, followed the next morning by his saltwater checkout near Harwood Island. He was now legal to fly the BC coast in his own floatplane.

Wally spent his subsequent years flying throughout the south coast, to logging camps and remote locations. After a storm on Powell Lake damaged his airplane, he moved the Luscombe to Cranberry Lake, where the airplane was better protected from the wind. Six other aircraft were already based on the tiny lake.

Powell Lake remained the main floatplane base in the region, including service by Queen Charlotte Airlines flying huge twin-engine biplanes. Later, Pacific Coastal Airlines opened a floatplane base on Powell Lake.

Cranberry Lake is so tiny, it could be considered a pond. But Wally found it adequate for his Luscombe.

"Lots of room, if you operated the right way. But I wouldn't takeoff with a full load of fuel and a passenger. It was either one or the other, not both."

Wally visited logging camps regularly, often transporting workers who needed to fly in or out. When flying north, he'd often refuel at Sullivan Bay or Alert Bay. Many of his flights were to an active logging operation up Seymour Inlet, one of the least traveled waterways near Queen Charlotte Strait. His flights often took him up the big inlets of the BC coast, including Knight, Bute, and Toba. Routinely, he'd land his Luscombe on the Unwin Lakes near Tenedos Bay to go fishing.

Wally remembers an elaborate logging camp on Vancouver Bay in Jervis Inlet as being particularly challenging. Closer to home, he regularly visited a logging operation at Jim Brown Creek, at the head of Powell Lake. The camp on Goat Lake provided reason for extra caution, with an obstacle course of mostly-submerged tree stumps.

Wally has watched Powell River Airport grow over the decades, through its transition from a gravel strip to a longer paved runway used by a succession of regional airlines. Meanwhile, he built up flying time in his Luscombe and other floatplanes, including a Beech 18 on floats, a Grumman Goose, and the unique twin-engine Cessna "Crane," with its large fabric-covered wing that twisted under load.

"Scared you half to death to see that wing twist during maneuvers, if you didn't know what was happening," relates Wally.

Regarding glassy water: "It's one of your enemies when you land on floats," he says. "You'll loose your depth perception, so sometimes you have to crowd in close to shore to use your peripheral vision as an aid. Then just setup a good rate of decent and fly it right on.

"Takeoffs can also be tricky when it's glassy, because it's harder to break the suction on the floats. With the Luscombe, one of the techniques on a lake as small as Cranberry is to get the nose up as high as possible on the takeoff run. When it feels right, push the stick forward and crack 15 degrees of flaps to jump up on the step, and then back on the stick to get airborne.

"You can also use the Luscombe's second notch of flaps (30 degrees) during takeoff to pump the airplane off the step and into the air. Or you may need to save your bacon with a quick pump of flaps to leapfrog over a log. It doesn't take much of a chunk of wood to take the bottom right off your floats. In Lois Lake, up near old Camp B where the fish farm is now, there were stumps everywhere, just below the waterline. Tough place to operate on floats."

Wally recalls plenty of weather-related situations that caused concern. The summer logging "show" at Rainbow Creek up Seymour Inlet was one of his frequent destinations. This relatively untraveled route was a place where winds could play havoc.

"There was a fire in the logging camp, and I was involved in bringing in replacement equipment. When it was time to leave, after four days at the camp, the super was putting pressure on me to get going. But a storm was moving through. When I began to taxi, the tailwind increased the farther I went out from shore. I could read the water and see the gusts coming, so I was trying to keep the wind on the tail, which is important in tailwinds. I kept looking out the back windows, trying to take the gusts right on the rear. But after a while, you get a little careless. So I missed one, and when it hit, I swapped ends. The outside float started to bury, and instinctively I tried to stop the swing with the rudders. Now I was looking right into the wind, so I punched it and bounced airborne in the next gust. Then I pushed the stick forward to level off just above the water with plenty of airspeed.

"Unfortunately, that wasn't the end of it, since I needed to go to Sullivan Bay to take on fuel. The landing was dicey in those gusty winds, and the takeoff at Sullivan was interesting too."

When I asked Wally to compare today's flight environment with the one he experienced during the 1950s and 60s, he quickly brought up the subject of radio communications.

"Things weren't as regimented then. Standard traffic pattern circuits and regulation turns made up for the lack of radio communications."

If it's true that experience is the best teacher, then Wally is well taught. Flying eras have come and gone, each with its special kind of excitement. Wally's era of flying was one of the most exciting of all.

* * * * *

One evening, a friend from California calls me from Williams Lake. He's homeward bound, living his dream – a solo flight adventure to Alaska. John teaches aviation at Mount San Antonio College, where I supervised the aeronautics department for 25 years, and I'm excited to see him. I'm also anxious to learn about his experiences at Canadian airports during the flight to and from Alaska. We meet the following morning at Powell River Airport.

John has spent two weeks exploring Alaska, camping under his wing (a Cessna 172) and exploring the most aviation-friendly state in the U.S. Alaskans feel deeply indebted to those who fly. Many sites can only be accessed by air.

John's airplane is packed with camping gear, including a motorized bike that is jammed into the baggage compartment. John has a lot to report, including the numerous weather challenges he faced along the way.

Once he arrived in Alaska, John was able to fly the coast north from Sitka, a route that is often blocked by a stubborn marine layer of clouds that persists in that area. He visited several destinations that I recommended to him from my previous visits to Alaska, including Sitka, Chandalar Lake, and the elaborate airport campground at Fairbanks.

John is an audiovisual junkie, and has produced some outstanding video material in both professional and personal formats. This time he has outdone himself, flying with a windshield mounted camera to capture the panoramic scenery of Alaska. I'm sure he'll make good use of it with his aviation students back in California.

A few hours later, we sit on the aft deck of the Bayliner, bobbing in the northwest bay at Mitlenatch Island, eating lunch and getting ready to go ashore. John is an experienced international aviator, flying regularly into Mexico as part of a volunteer medical support team. I'm interested in his overall impressions of flying in Canada.

"British Columbia is one of my favorite places," he says. "I've traveled here before, but only by RV. My first landing was in Cranbrook, and it was remarkable that I didn't have to talk to Customs, except by phone. From Cranbrook, I flew non-stop to Prince George, the longest flight of the entire trip, 380 nautical miles."

I ask John to compare Nav Canada's flight plan procedures to those in the States, and he expresses his overall comfort with the Canadian system.

"Of course, VFR flight plans are mandatory here, and I'm not used to that. The biggest concern I had was forgetting to close a flight plan, but I got more comfortable as I saw how helpful all Nav Canada facilities are with the closing of flight plans."

When I ask about weather briefing support, an important component of flight planning, John notes some contrasting aspects of the Canadian weather briefing process. Since he is an aviation weather expert (teaches the subject in California), I'm particularly interested in his opinion on this topic.

"Telephone weather briefings are excellent – friendly, patient personnel who are very knowledgeable, for the most part. But I also encountered kiosks at several airports, and they weren't user-friendly, at least not for me. These Internet links are a great concept, but they use an awkward touchpad system that I've never encountered before. Worse than that, the slow speed of the Internet connection is frustrating, using a dial-up interface. If you're downloading a weather map, it seems to take forever. Even more annoying to me was the fact that there was a weather briefer right next door to the kiosk, but you can only talk to him by radio in flight. So there he was with all the information I needed, and here I was struggling with this awkward kiosk. I'm grateful for the service, but some improvements, especially in the computer system's connection speed, would be nice."

From Prince George, John flew his Cessna 172 to Prince Rupert and then on to Sitka, where he cleared Customs into Alaska. On the way home, he entered Canada at Whitehorse, flew south to Watson Lake, and then to Mackenzie at the south end of the "Trench." This is the most common route for small aircraft flying in the northern Canadian Rockies.

On his trip south, after spending the night at Williams Lake, he flew over the spectacular mountain terrain that leads to the head of Jervis Inlet and then to Powell River. Along this route, he snapped photos to capture the enduring beauty of mountains that drop directly into the sea.

"After a trip like this one, it's hard to top the beauty of everything I've seen," says John. "But after my brief time here in Powell River, this is about as close to a spiritual experience as it gets."

John didn't need to say that, but I'm glad he did.

◊ ◊ ◊ ◊ ◊ ◊ ◊

Chapter 10

Canadian Shield

I t's a part of Canada that captured my attention before I saw it. Reading Farley Mowat's adventurous accounts of Arctic Canada, I become enthralled with the far north. The Canadian Shield (sometimes called the Precambrian Shield or Laurentian Shield) is the glacier-scoured area that covers most of northern and eastern Canada, including the Barrens regions where Mowat concentrated his travels and writing (*People of the Deer*, 1951; *Walking on the Land*, 2000; *High Latitudes*, 2003; *No Man's River*, 2004).

The bedrock of the continent shows through the thin layer of soil of the Canadian Shield. Lakes are scattered so plentifully that travel in most areas is impossible, except by airplane (usually on floats or skis) or by laborious journeys on winter ice roads. The lakes are remnants of the last ice age, and the shallow stratum is older still. This area has one of the oldest swaths of exposed bedrock on earth.

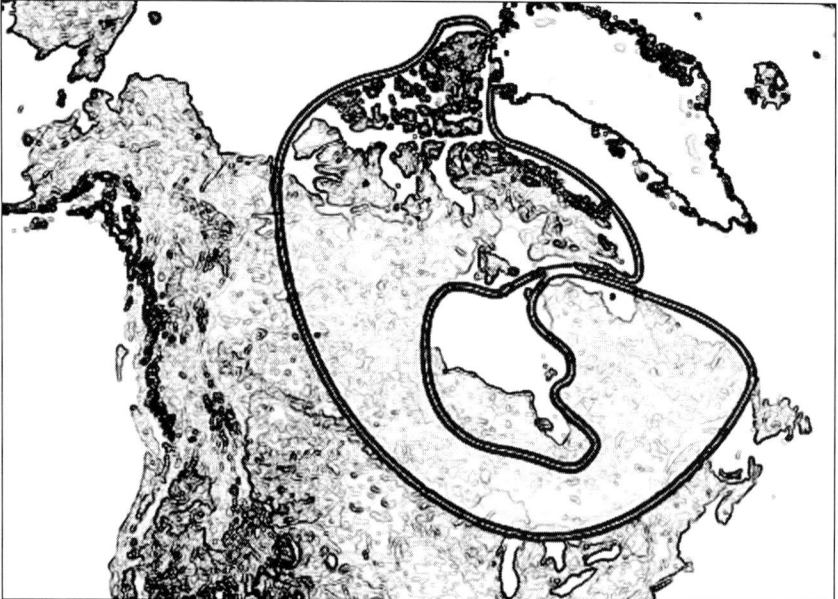

My first view of the Canadian Shield occurred on a flight northeast from Medicine Hat (Alberta). I intended to fly 600 miles through Saskatchewan, past Saskatoon and Prince Albert, to Malcolm Island on Reindeer Lake. But only an hour after leaving Medicine Hat, the weather began to deteriorate. Fair weather clouds were building into towering cumulus, creating an unstable sky full of moderate turbulence. As usual during the onset of turbulence, Margy and I quickly agree to end the flight at the nearest convenient location. In this case, it's a grass airstrip right off the nose of the Arrow and perfectly positioned for a descent from our cruising altitude of 7500 feet.

Farmers' fields spread in all directions in precise grid lines from the highway intersection adjacent to the airport and the small town of Eatonia, Saskatchewan, population 474. A huge grain elevator is the town's most prominent structure.

We drop down for an overnight stay, prepared to camp by our airplane, next to the grass runway. It's a relief to get out of the turbulence and onto firm ground.

Before setting up our tent, we walk to a nearby hangar to seek permission to camp. It's a formality that's far from necessary at an airport like this, but it always makes me feel better to find someone who seems to be in charge. The hangar we select is the private shop of a local pilot who has found his personal safe haven in this small town. The elaborate shop includes an entire wall of hand tools, organized into shadow boxes.

"Do you think it's okay to pitch a tent by our airplane tonight?" I ask.

"Oh, sure, sure," he says. "No one will care."

Since his is the only car parked at the airport, it seems a logical answer.

Robert does more than calm my concerns. He insists on serving as our personal tour guide for the evening. As we put away our Coleman stove and repack the dishes after dinner, he drives up to our tent in his big Buick.

"Wanna ride around a bit? Got some things to show you," he offers.

The tour gives us a glimpse of the local lifestyle on the Canadian prairie. We rumble along back roads that divide the Canola fields, stopping at the homes of several of Robert's friends, including a visit

to the house of a local artist. It doesn't make any difference that the
artist isn't at home, since the house is unlocked.

"He won't mind if I take you through to see his carvings," says
Robert. "Look at them– aren't they great?"

The wood carvings are elaborate, and the house is beautiful. So
is the Saskatoon Berry pie that Robert's wife serves us at their house.
When we arrive back at the airport, we climb into our tent for the
night, and don't even consider locking the door.

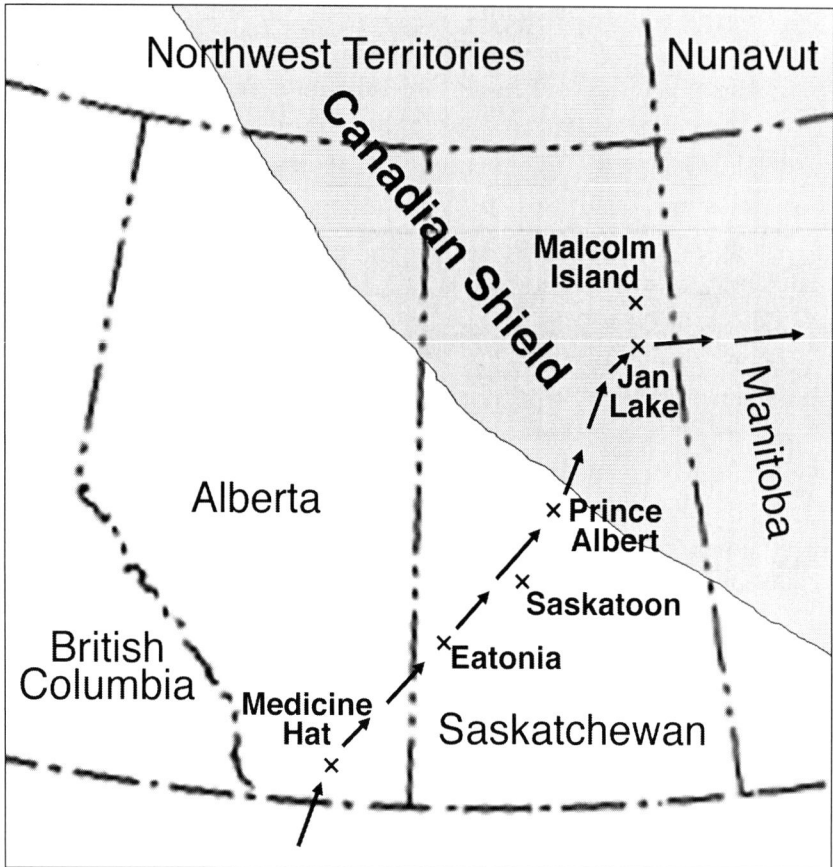

* * * * *

The next morning, we are up early in an attempt to beat the prairie's
typical rising summer convection currents and the accompanying turbulence. I make a takeoff that combines the techniques used on grass
fields (nose up and airborne early) and short fields (hold the nose
down in the thick air near ground level, then establish the best angle

of climb). Such a combination is usually futile, since you're better off following one procedure or the other. On this rutted grassy field, my on-the-spot combination of flying techniques makes for a safe but bouncy departure.

We fly over Saskatoon, stopping at Prince Albert for fuel. Almost immediately after getting airborne again, we enter the boundary of the Canadian Shield, marked by an abrupt change in the terrain. We watch endless lines of lakes pass below us, pocketed within bedrock that extends in all directions.

Our destination is the same as the previous day, Malcolm Island, but once again we face mid-day turbulence. Scattered thunderstorms rise around us, prompting another unscheduled stop. While Margy flies, I thumb through the Canadian *Flight Supplement*, matching names with likely looking airports on the chart. Jan Lake gets my attention. The runway is a reasonable length (3150 feet) for this low elevation (1100 feet), although it will take cool, dense air in the early morning to make a safe takeoff. The runway is a mix of gravel and dirt, but the *Flight Supplement's* airfield diagram is what motivates me. The airstrip sits right next to the lake, a perfect camping location. With the lake so near, our overnight stay should include a free bath.

Soon after landing, we set up our tent, and I decide to try out two recent additions to our camping gear. First, I plug in an electric air pump, using the DC socket in the Arrow. The cord slithers out the door, down the wing to the air mattress. I look forward to the luxury of pumping up the mattress without using the older foot pump.

The electric pump hums softly, but the air mattress does not seem to inflate. The mattress's rubber top quivers from the flow of air, but looks almost the same after five minutes. I begin to worry about the airplane's battery. This would be a bad place to be without a starter. Maybe an electric air pump is not such a good idea.

I put away the new pump and inflate the air mattress with the old-fashioned foot pump. The mattress is fully inflated in just a few minutes. So much for technology.

Now I try the new electric fan. This time, I'm using double-A batteries to drive the tiny motor. The theory is that the fan will cool the tent on warm evenings and also keep the bugs away. Since nights in northern Canada are seldom warm enough to require a fan, control of mosquitoes and black flies is the only real advantage. While I test the fan outside the tent, I notice several bugs flying effortlessly in front of the humming blade. After a few minutes, with bugs seemingly unaffected by the meager flow of air, the fan dies. It seemed like a good idea at the time. (So did pullover mosquito net hats that we tested once and have never used since. But we still carry them in our airplane survival kit everywhere we go, just in case.)

After dinner, Margy and I walk to the lake, but forego our bath. The water is clogged with lily pads. So we sit contentedly on the small dock and watch the summer sun dip down towards the horizon. At this high latitude, the sun will set in the northwest and then slide just below the horizon until 4 am, when it will rise again in the northeast.

Back at the airplane, I decide to walk the runway before calling it a night. In preparation for takeoff the next morning, it's a good idea to check out the unpaved strip for ruts and rocks that may not have been seen during landing. That's particularly true at a remote and rarely-used runway like this one. Tonight, our Arrow is the only airplane here.

I decide to combine my airstrip inspection with an evening jog, so I start down the runway at a slow trot. All is clear of stones, so I don't need to interrupt my run to pick up debris. At the far end, I pause to check my watch before starting back. I'm amazed at the time – 11:10.

It feels like early evening, the still-bright sky adding to that perception. Here I am – jogging along a remote runway on the Canadian Shield at eleven o'clock at night, headed back to my tent for a short night's sleep. Farley Mowat would love it.

* * * * *

Another summer trip to the Canadian Shield begins in Los Angeles and takes me north through Calgary and Edmonton to Yellowknife. Again, I experience the sudden transition to a multitude of lakes puddled in endless bedrock near Fort Smith, on the border of the Northwest Territories.

On this trip, the takeoff from Edmonton City Centre Airport is memorable. This small but busy airport, unlike Edmonton International's two-mile-long runways, sits strategically near downtown, providing easy access to the city. (Soon after our visit, the airport will be shut down, due to increasing safety concerns about takeoffs and landings over the city.)

We choose a hotel in town and enjoy our stay. The next day is hot and sunny (at least by Edmonton standards), but the 5900-foot runway will be long enough for the Arrow. At 2200 feet elevation, we should have plenty of asphalt even at mid-day, so we delay our departure until near noon.

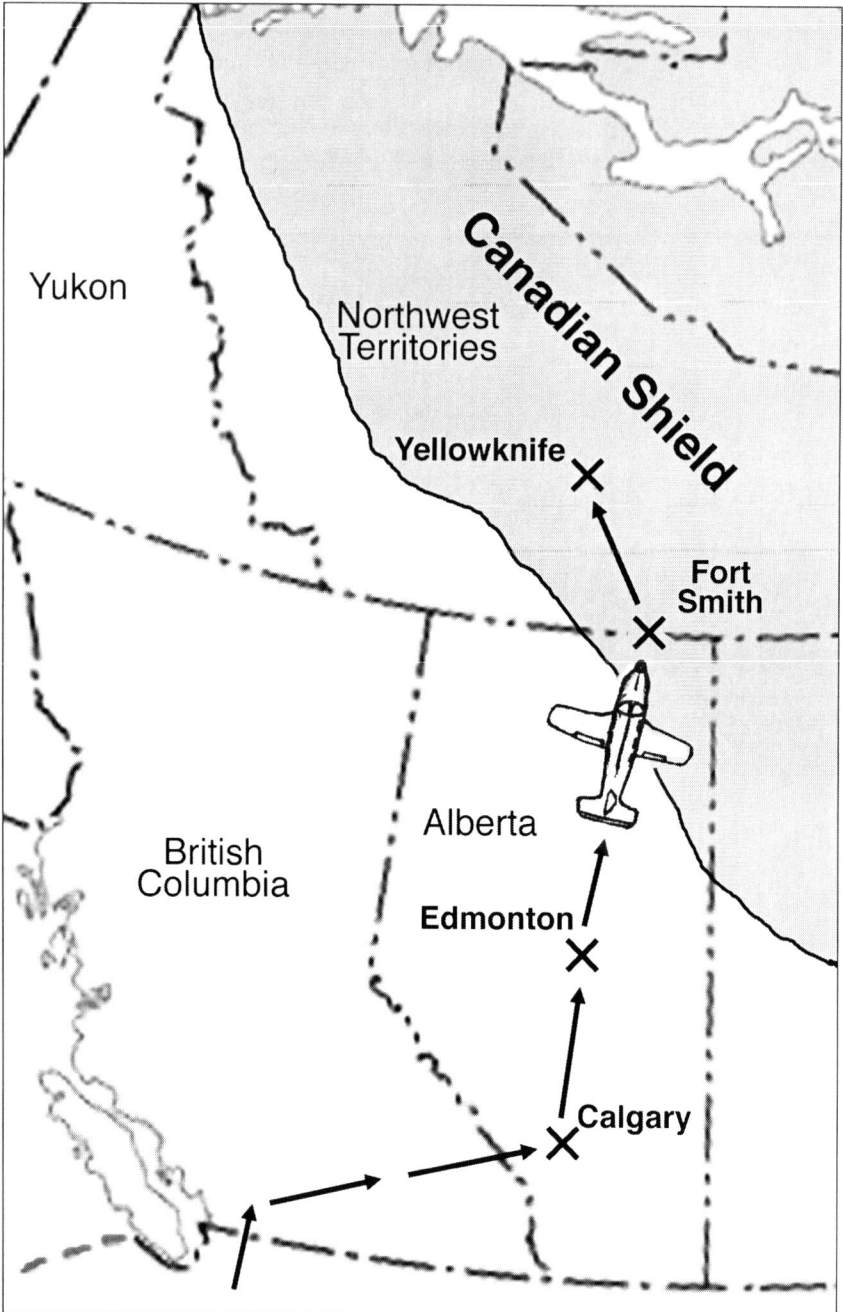

Margy prepares the Arrow for the takeoff, and neither of us thinks much about the thin-air conditions, since the runway is plenty long. On the other hand, for our long Canadian trips, we load the Arrow to maximum gross weight, and now it is the middle of the day. I also think about the numbers of hours on our engine, now approaching overhaul limits. It's a good engine, but its advanced hours equate to reduced compression, a problem that has begun to show up during maximum weight takeoffs. Still, 5900 feet is a lot of runway.

Margy selects two notches of flaps (20 degrees), and completes the pre-departure checklist. When the control tower clears us for takeoff, she positions the Arrow on the runway centerline. She pushes the throttle full forward while holding the brakes, standard short-field takeoff procedure. This is not a short field, but on hot days it never hurts to treat runways with respect.

When Margy releases the brakes, the Arrow accelerates sluggishly, but there is still a lot of pavement ahead of us. As the airspeed creeps up to our normal 60 mile-per-hour rotation speed, we watch the end of the runway looming in the windshield. We break ground well before the pavement ends, but without the firm upward leap expected with two notches of flaps. I watch Margy lower the nose to pick up speed in the denser air lying immediately above the runway; perfect form for a short field. Then we begin our climb, as high-rise buildings line up in the departure path directly ahead.

Normally, it would be a straight path up and over the buildings, but this takeoff needs special treatment. We are barely climbing. Margy reaches down to retract the landing gear, while I stay focused on the instruments and the buildings ahead. There is no need to intervene, since Margy is handling the situation perfectly, but my feet remain poised over the rudder pedals, and my hand could be on the yoke in an instant. I remain perfectly straight in my seat, not wanting to move even the slightest. My smallest movement might disrupt our rate of climb. Margy sits straight up too, and I know she is focused and working this climb to the maximum. She leaves the flaps extended, as is best in such a marginal climb. There would be a momentary loss of lift if she retracted the flaps, and we can't afford it.

Margy doesn't ask me to take the airplane from her, as she might do in other critical situations. I'm glad, since even a quick transition of pilots on the controls could be costly today. We inch our way upward.

"I'm going around those buildings," she says quietly.

"Good," I reply curtly.

It's a lot better than going through them.

She banks the airplane ever so gently, being careful to sacrifice as little lift as possible during the maneuver. A building passes barely off to our left, the Arrow well below its top. Then the departure crisis passes, as flat terrain stretches out before us.

Margy retracts one notch of flaps, and then another. She reduces the throttle to the cruise-climb setting, adjusts the prop lever for 2500 RPM, leans the fuel mixture for 12 gallons per hour, and turns off the electric fuel pump. Then she glances at me with a strange let's-have-a-talk look.

"We're getting a new engine," she says.

"Okay, that will be nice."

With the adrenaline-producing takeoff now behind us, suddenly we relax.

"You also get a three-bladed prop," she adds.

It has really never been in contention. We've planned on a new engine at the end of this trip. The three-bladed prop is a modification we've discussed and pretty well agreed upon, since it will provide better climb performance. It's "our" airplane, not "mine," so when Margy talks about "my" prop, I know what she means. This takeoff has been all-too memorable.

"I'll take a new prop too," I reply.

* * * * *

On another trip, returning from the Arctic Ocean, we fly south from Inuvik, passing over an extensive section of the Canadian Shield. We land at Norman Wells for fuel, where we find giant oil refineries lining the bank of the Mackenzie River. Even the original native name for this town translates as "where there is oil." We shake our heads when we pay a substantially higher price for gas here than we have experienced on the entire trip.

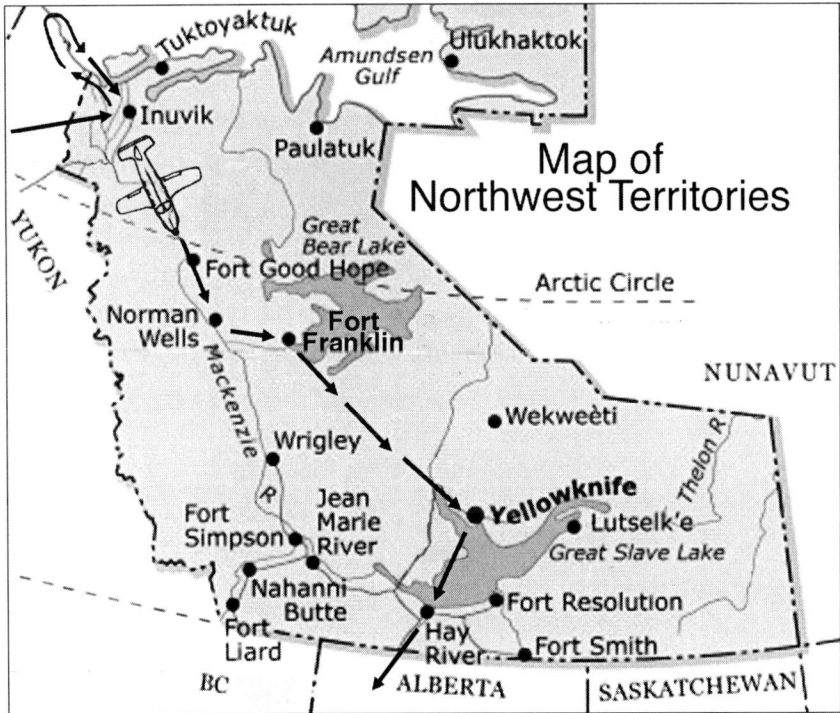

Map of Northwest Territories

It's a quick hop (0.9 hours) to Fort Franklin (recently renamed Deline) on the west arm of Great Bear Lake, the world's eighth largest lake. We camp next to our airplane, with the First Nations village within easy walking distance.

The next morning, we fly over the barren Canadian Shield country that lies between the two biggest lakes in northern Canada, Great Bear and Great Slave Lake. We land at Yellowknife for fuel, then continue south across Great Slave Lake, landing at Hay River to top off our tanks again. We're not sure where we'll find our next gas, so Hay River makes sense as a fuel stop – that is, until we get on the ground. My logbook remarks at Hay River cryptically state: "Nasty black flies. Beat feet!"

These flies are beyond nasty. When we get out of the airplane, they swarm all around us. The fuel attendant swats at them as he fills our tanks.

"How far to town?" I ask, hoping it is a short walk to lunch.

"Don't do it," mumbles the attendant, as he hastily writes up our credit card receipt.

"What do you mean?"

"Don't do it," he repeats. "You'll regret it."

I look around me. The black flies swarm in clouds, although they don't seem to be biting yet. The town may not be far, but it could be a most unpleasant walk.

We quickly get back into the airplane and slam the door. Then we crank up the engine, and beat feet.

◊ ◊ ◊ ◊ ◊ ◊

Chapter 11

Alert Bay

I stumble out onto the deck of the float cabin in the muted dawn of early morning. Stars twinkle faintly in the west, while the east is dominated by the silhouette of Goat Island and the brightening sky.

When I'm ready to go, I'm simply ready, no matter what kind of flight is anticipated. I'm the same way when flying on an airliner – ready to go before dawn. I suppose it's due to my heightened sense of anticipation, although stepping onto the deck in the wee hours of morning is not unusual for me. I love to witness the transition from dark to dawn. Usually I check out the pre-dawn constellations and slip back to bed, content that the stars are right where they are supposed to be.

The glow to the east, behind Goat Island, indicates that 4 am is approaching. The Summer Triangle (Vega, Deneb, and Altair) lies directly overhead, verifying the hour. I know my constellations, and I can tell time fairly well with their assistance. Of course, it only works when you take the season into account. Late May with the Summer Triangle overhead – about 4 o'clock.

I step back inside and shine my flashlight on the clock on the bookshelf – 4:15. John would be proud of me. He can tell time at least as accurately as this in the middle of the day, even under a cloudy sky. Using the stars is easier for me.

I try going back to bed, but I'm fully awake now. I lie there thinking about the route of flight, the radar facilities along the way, and the path we'll follow home. Finally, I give into my wide-awake state and go back downstairs. I begin to pack up for the trip to town and then north along the coast to Alert Bay.

Margy does not awaken easily, although she readily accepts my decision to get an early start. The earlier we leave, the sooner we'll be back to our float cabin. She too loves flying, but leaving our floating home is even harder for her. Both of us are enchanted with this cabin, and to leave Hole in the Wall, even to go flying, takes concerted effort.

* * * * *

We motor through First Narrows, dodging the early morning flotsam. As we enter the North Sea, we pass a crew boat headed in the opposite direction. Another kilometre farther south, the sun pops out from behind Goat Island. I glance at my watch – 6:15.

We stop at the condo to pick up some additional flying gear, and then we're off to the airport. We're ahead of schedule, but possibly too early for the fog to have lifted farther north at Alert Bay.

Our takeoff is to the west, breaking ground a few minutes before 8 o'clock. We climb straight out over Harwood Island, making our initial ATC contact with Comox Terminal as we leave 2000 feet. I normally prefer radar "flight following" when flying VFR, and the radar facility at Comox covers our path for the first 50 kilometres. After that, we'll be on our own the rest of the way to Alert Bay.

For us, this is an extended overwater flight, although local pilots would take it in stride. Below us lies a mix of water and islands, with mountainous shoreline on both sides – not a very hospitable environment for an emergency landing in an airplane on wheels. So we fly at 6500 feet to provide plenty of gliding distance and lots of time to let someone know if we encounter problems. Of course, aircraft engines are extremely reliable, but it never hurts to be prepared. We don't carry a life raft, but we have our yellow life vests tucked in the back seat, within easy reach.

The morning is nearly cloudless, with visibility at least 30 kilometres. Passing over Savary Island, we settle into cruise. Hansen Field, a cute little airstrip on the south end of Cortes Island, is directly in front of us. This is a private airport, but there's a phone number to call if you can handle landing on a 1700 feet mix of gravel and grass.

Farther north, the land and sea is replaced by cloud, a low marine layer covering most of the area. This could last all the way to Alert Bay. The low overcast at Port Hardy is forecast to burn off quickly this morning, but the stratus could hang around longer than expected.

On my right, Bute Inlet cuts into the mountains, looking tiny and routine. The deep fjord passes under my wing, a ridge of glaciated peaks rising beyond it. From my one visit to Bute in a boat, I know the inlet is far from minuscule. The scale, viewed from an altitude of 6500 feet, is misleading. It miniaturizes the majestic beauty of the coast. From up here, the rugged grandeur that you get at ground-level can be easily missed. You see more, you see farther, but it's not up-close and personal.

Before drifting out of Comox's communication area, I request the latest Port Hardy weather, and it's relayed to me immediately: "1700 few, 2300 broken, 4500 broken."

Port Hardy lies 35 kilometres beyond Alert Bay, and multiple layers of clouds can make descents impossible during VFR operations. Additionally, Canadian flight rules regarding "VFR-over-the-top" (above a solid layer of clouds) are more restrictive than in the States. At the moment, I can't recall exactly how these rules differ, and this isn't the best time to fumble through the regulations booklet stuffed inside my chart bag. Although there are still holes in the clouds below us, a solid layer of white looms ahead. Regardless of the rules, why waste gas needlessly if we're not going to get into the airport.

So with the GPS showing Alert Bay only 40 miles in front of us, we reverse course and head back to Campbell River. While I talk to "Campbell Radio," Margy descends for a left downwind entry and a landing on Runway 29.

By 9:30, we're eating breakfast in the airport cafe, planning out the rest of our day. We're disappointed regarding our missed visit to Alert Bay, but we'll be back to Powell River before noon, with the whole day still ahead of us. By early afternoon, we'll be back home on our float. Alert Bay can wait for another day.

* * * * *

The next time Margy and I try this route, Port Hardy's weather report indicates that the typical early morning clouds are already beginning to dissipate. Of course, Alert Bay could still be overcast, but the conditions looks good. High pressure dominates the area, with a forecast for clear skies that will give way to clouds soon after sunset.

We fly northwest over Johnstone Strait, watching the tumbling currents below us. Several boats brave the turbulent water, now at mid-tide; they won't tackle the toughest stretches (such as Seymour Narrows) until slack tide.

The clouds ahead are scattered as far as the eye can see. But the view is without any significant patches that might prevent a VFR descent.

Alert Bay is one of the bigger airstrips up the coast from Powell River. Its runway stretches 2900 feet, with clear approaches on both ends. Only Port Hardy has more pavement. A smaller asphalt runway at Port McNeil, 2400 feet in length, is marginal for a fully loaded Piper

Arrow, although the airfield has a longer alternate gravel strip that we'd prefer to avoid with our low-slung propeller. After Port Hardy, the next northerly airport is at Bella Bella. In this region, there's a lot of water and inhospitable terrain for any aircraft other than a floatplane.

Approaching Alert Bay, I begin the descent and enter the traffic pattern (with no traffic) on a modified right base leg for Runway 27. I line up on a five-mile final and slide down the approach path, lowering the landing gear and adding flaps. I run the *GUMPS* checklist out loud.

"Gas – fullest tank. Undercarriage – three green. Mixture – full rich, with the pump. Prop – full forward. Seatbelts – latched. Landing checklist complete."

Our landing is uphill, with plenty of stopping distance, if you don't waste the first part of the runway. But there's a drop-off at the far end, so it gets your attention. Radio towers, including two off to the left side of the approach end of Runway 27 encourage pilots to maintain centerline.

Two decades ago, Margy and I camped on this airport and visited the cultural centre in town. I remember the walk downhill and the slow climb back up to the airport. And I remember a town that seemed to be on the leading edge of a tourist boom that I expect to encounter today.

But when I pull off the runway into the parking ramp, the level of activity is minimal. In fact, only one Cessna 152 is parked here, and it is covered by a tarp. Mounds of dirt are piled along the far edge of the ramp, indicating either the destruction of old facilities or the birth of buildings not yet constructed. A pay phone sits outside a small, boarded-up airport terminal building. The overall atmosphere is one of economic decay, not uncommon in the world of private aviation these days.

We hike down the road to town, past brightly colored houses, including one with a long picket fence painted a bright violet. We pass two boys digging with tiny shovels in a pile of dirt, their yellow toy tractors poised nearby.

The village below is a bit of a surprise. The tourism boom has obviously not arrived. This is a warm July day, and the ferry is on its way in, but the streets are not crowded. The few tourists who walk along the road have only a small number of places to visit, including two gift shops and several small cafes. The view looking out over the harbour is spectacular, but there aren't many folks here to enjoy it.

A wooden boardwalk, nicely maintained, is an attractive place to walk, until it abruptly ends near the ferry terminal, where an old building lies in decay alongside the road. Tourists walking back and forth from the ferry terminal are forced out onto the road. We hustle the 50 metres to the concrete walkway at the terminal's parking lot, to avoid becoming an Alert Bay statistic.

The boom I anticipated is nonexistent, and I'm both pleased and saddened. I'm pleased for us on this July day, but I'm saddened by the economic impact on the community. The large abandoned cannery at the far end of the harbour tells part of the story, but why hasn't this town become a popular travel destination? All seems right with this village, and ready to develop, but the retail infrastructure is missing. So are the tourists.

Where is the world's largest totem pole? Alert Bay is famous for these towering carvings. I remember visiting a spectacular pole during our trip here 20 years ago. But I also remember seeing a larger museum then, on the other side of the road. Maybe the giant pole (and museum) is back down the road, although the road we hiked during our descent from the airport seems to be the same one we walked on our previous visit. We couldn't have missed such a huge pole during today's walk down from the airport. (Later, I research the world's largest totem pole and learn that it stands at the cultural center rather than at the museum, a hike of 2 kilometres from the ferry terminal. Apparently, we didn't walk far enough to see the 53-metre totem this time around.)

After lunch at an uncrowded cafe, Margy and I hoof it along the road, back past where we descended from the airport, trying to locate the big totem pole. We never find it, but we do discover something more magnificent – a cemetery with many smaller totem poles in a serene setting that is both beautiful and eerie. The Namgis Burial Ground is a sight to behold.

As we sit on a bench across the street from the cemetery, I watch mid-level clouds rolling in from the west. The next storm is approaching faster than expected, with the only remaining area of blue sky now far to the south. It's time to climb the hill back to the airport and depart while conditions remain acceptable.

As we huff-and-puff our way back up the hill, we pass the community hall, now closed. It's further evidence that all is not well here, at least economically. Sometimes the most beautiful and accessible locations on the BC coast miss the tourism boom. For now, this town is preserved from change, and that is not necessarily a bad thing. Maybe the locals aren't missing anything they would value. Meanwhile, Alert Bay sits relatively untouched by the fast pace of the new century.

◊ ◊ ◊ ◊ ◊ ◊ ◊

Chapter 12

San Juan Islands

The San Juan Islands are a must-visit for any pilot in the area. I've landed at Friday Harbor several times and camped on the island. The airport at Lopez Island is also nice, but I've never left the airplane because it's a long walk to town. Orcas Island is a great pilot getaway, where I once strolled to the beach and spent an afternoon sunbathing and reading in this relaxed island setting.

Now, for a return visit before the tourist crunch of mid-summer arrives, Margy and I perform our preflight inspection of the Arrow at Bellingham Airport in the early morning light of mid-May. Margy does the exterior part of the preflight, while I prepare the Arrow's cockpit and ready our charts.

"Found a couple of things," she reports.

If you ever need an aircraft preflight with a professional level of quality, Margy would be an excellent candidate. She walks me around the airplane, pointing out a missing screw in the nose cowl's air inlet and some deteriorated sealant along the edge of one of the fuel tank joints. I pull out my pocket notebook to log these squawks for attention later, but I am more concerned with her discovery of a hydraulic leak at the left main landing gear brake fitting. A drop of sticky red hydraulic fluid covers the end of the fitting, with a mostly-dried small puddle of fluid on the pavement.

When you let an airplane sit for a month, as we have because of a visit to Los Angeles by airliner, idle equipment deteriorates as it sits. Nothing is worse than leaving an airplane inactive, and this brake leak proves it. This airplane is flyable, but the leak will require attention soon.

"Once we get aboard, we can check the brakes better," I suggest. "As soon as we get rolling, you can check to make sure both sides respond properly."

This, of course, implies that Margy will do the initial taxiing, as is almost always the case. After a period of inactivity such as this, I'll have plenty of time to check over the engine gauges as she taxis.

We taxi without incident ("Brakes feel fine," Margy reports), but run into a problem during the pre-departure checklist at the end of the runway.

"The electric trim is inop, at least in the aft direction," Margy reports, as she tries to run the trim switch to the takeoff position. "Seems okay going forward."

"Set it manually," I suggest. "We'll see what happens in flight."

It's not unusual for the electric trim switch, neglected by inactivity, to refuse to cooperate.

We depart Bellingham at a high rate of climb in the thick, cool morning air. Margy levels off at 2500 feet and points the nose across the southern islands of the San Juans, cruising above scattered stratocumulus. Looking farther north, where this same archipelago merges into the Gulf Islands of British Columbia, the "strato-cu" seem a bit thicker.

"Electric trim is back to normal," says Margy.

Things don't usually fix themselves, but this airplane's electric trim system is an exception, probably a victim of congealed grease. With the backup manual trim operational, it's not a safety concern. Now, with the electric trim working normally, it's certainly not worth worrying about.

"Want to report it to maintenance?" I joke.

The finicky electric trim system is not something we want messed with. It's the kind of subsystem that could get a lot worse with too much tinkering.

"Yah, right," she laughs. "If it ain't broke, don't fix it."

It's a quick 25 nautical miles to Friday Harbor from Bellingham. The air inside the cockpit is warm enough for T-shirts and shorts, and I even need to open the Arrow's air vents for comfort – first time this year.

Margy releases the yoke and lets the airplane fly itself for a few moments, while she snaps some photos of the islands below us. I tune in for the pre-recorded weather report at Friday Harbor.

"Do you think the temperature is really minus seventeen?" I ask. The automated weather report is obviously in error.

"Feels like about plus seventeen to me," replies Margy. Aviation weather reports, even in the States, are issued in Celsius.

Margy offers me the yoke, and I take control of the airplane to begin the descent for Friday Harbor. I maneuver downward between scattered clouds and onto the downwind leg for a landing to the north.

After landing, you can make a left turn off to the small commercial terminal for charter aircraft and airplanes requiring U.S. Customs inspections. Pilots can fly direct to Friday Harbor from Canada, but you'll need to provide two hours advance notice. Delays in the arrival of Customs authorities at your aircraft can be expected during the busy summer months, since the officials must drive from the ferry terminal in town.

We exit the runway to the right, and park in the spacious area designated for transient aircraft. From this spot on the northeast corner of the airport, it's a quick walk to town, where we plan to rent bikes at Island Bicycles. We haven't made reservations (which are recommended in the middle of summer), but there should be plenty of bikes available today.

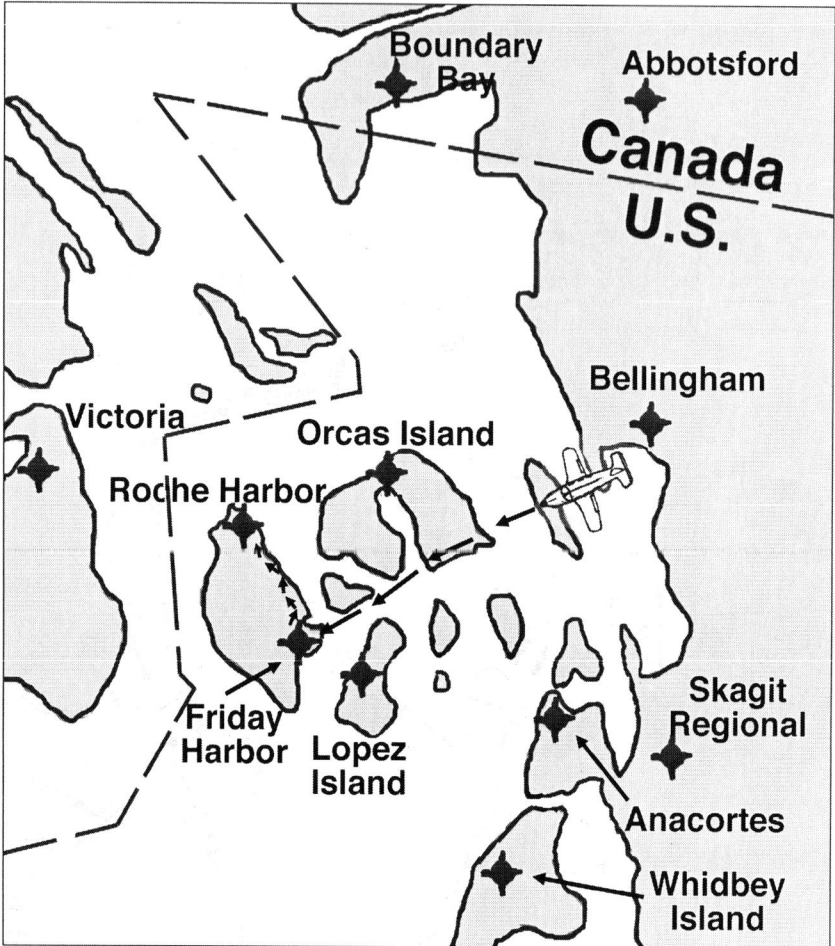

As we prepare the bicycle rental paperwork, the jovial attendant banters with us. He hovers over the counter, a middle-age-plus guy in T-shirt and shorts (like me). He seems pleasantly feisty (occasionally like me).

"Sign here," he says.

I scribble my signature while halfheartedly glancing at the four paragraphs above the signature line.

"Did you read what you signed?" he quips.

"Sure," I say. "All the normal stuff."

"You know, you just joined the Army."

"Oh, that's okay," I reply.

"Maybe we should invade Canada. We could steal all of their water."

I laugh, but I'm not sure what brought this on. Then I remember that I'm wearing my bright red *Canada* cap.

"Their lumber too," I say. "Oops, I forgot. We already did that."

It's not meant to be vengeful. Maybe a little more levity on the subject would be good for both countries.

"Here's a map," he says. "The arrows show where there are hills; the more arrows, the steeper it gets."

"Any bears?" I ask.

Margy gives me that look – the one that means to ease up a bit.

"No, but we've got a camel," he says. "Look for her, along with a white stallion, on the left side of the road to Roche Harbor."

"Are you serious?" I ask.

"Absolutely," he replies.

I'm not sure whether to believe him or not, but I'll be looking for a camel.

From the bike shop, we coast down the hill to the ferry terminal. At the waterfront, large construction cranes are maneuvering steel beams over a newly poured concrete foundation, probably for more condominiums or new stores. This town is growing fast, and more-so with the tourist season rapidly approaching. Springtime sounds – hammers pounding in the background – signal last minute attempts to meet construction deadlines.

After an early lunch at the Downrigger restaurant, a nice spot over-looking the harbour, we begin our bike trip across the island. The automobile traffic is heavier than I'd expect for this time of year, and it makes me wonder what it will be like during summer.

We maneuver our way out of town, uphill past the courthouse and onto Tucker Avenue that soon turns into Roche Harbor Road. Bike lanes alongside the road make me feel more comfortable in this heavy traffic.

It's a pretty ride, 15 kilometres to Roche Harbor, winding through grazing country, with sheep and cows, but no camel. We stop for a rest near a granite slope at the side of the road where bright orange poppies are in full bloom.

Some of the uphill sections of the road are steep enough to require Margy to walk her bike. On some of these grades, I walk with her. On others, I press on up the hills in low gear, waiting for her to catch up to me at the crest.

Shortly after stopping at a rest area with a picnic table provided specifically for bikers, I catch sight of a white stallion standing on the left side of the road. Beyond the stallion, right next to the road, a camel (named Mona) grazes contentedly. Mona's owner, who used to live in Egypt, always wanted a camel of her own. Now she has one – on a non-desert island called San Juan.

By now, it's 1 o'clock, and I'm beginning to wonder if we will make it to Roche Harbor in time to return to the bicycle shop before closing time at 5:30. The ride is not difficult, but there are plenty of hills to slow us down. My energy is fading, and I can imagine Margy's challenges, with her shorter legs, using lower gears. And these bike saddles aren't the most comfortable.

On the other hand, these seats are better than I am used to on our own bikes in Powell River. In fact, the contrast between these rental bikes (about $500 when new) and our Canadian Tire discount specials ($150) is very noticeable. When you buy cheap bikes, you get what you pay for.

It's a lot like our previous airplane engine (that we now call our "crappy engine"). We never realized how much of a problem that engine was until it died on us. Now our "new" (overhauled) engine burns almost no oil and never fouls the spark plugs. By contrast, the "crappy engine" was an oil hog from the very beginning, and we needed to run it overly lean to avoid fouled plugs. We didn't realize how bad it was until we got rid of it. Similarly, these rental bikes have smooth brakes that don't grab and screech, and shift levers that operate smoothly and efficiently. Our old discount bikes will never seem the same again, now referred to as our "crappy bikes."

We pause at a picturesque viewpoint overlooking Westcott Bay, oyster territory. The gentle downslope among the apple trees reminds me of a previous visit to British Camp (only two klicks from here), with similar gently sloping vistas overlooking Garrison Bay.

Good brakes and smooth shifting gears haven't solved our energy crisis. By the time we arrive at Roche Harbor (after 3 o'clock), it is apparent that we are short of both time and stamina to return to the bike shop before closing. That's one of the reasons they invented van-cabs.

Before dropping down the final hill into Roche Harbor, we stop at the private airport. This airstrip has come a long way in recent years, now smoothly paved (previously it was a gravel-grass mix) and 4200 feet long, although still only 30-feet wide – safe but daunting. The airstrip is PPR (prior permission required), but landing rights can be easily procured by telephone, if you're going to the Roche Harbor Resort (or say you are). The dogleg at the west end is now designated for transient parking, an improvement from the previous helter-skelter parking area in the sloping grass. It's a one-way-in, other-way-out strip, except in the strongest of wind conditions. Because of the upslope to the east, you land to the east and takeoff to the west.

We coast down the final hill to the harbour, past new construction that dots the entire settlement. Condos and new stores are sprouting up in typical Pacific Northwest get-ready-for-summer style. It's a last minute rush to see if things can be finished in time, which seems unlikely.

It appears that this small town is incapable of sustaining much more concrete sprawl. Although buildings are springing up everywhere, it's obvious that "everywhere" is located within a very narrow harbour. Like Lund, near our home in Powell River, this is the end of the highway. (Don't tell that to the residents of Lund, who insist it is the "beginning" of Highway 101.) Also like Lund, there is nowhere to park. Keep constructing, and then what? Already today, in mid-May, vehicles are circling like vultures, looking for parking spaces. I bet it will be fun in July.

We park our bikes and walk to the pier. Although a few dock spaces are vacant, the harbour is already nearly full. How will these docks be able to handle the increase in boat traffic during summer? The solution is probably found at nearby anchorages, with an onslaught of dinghies motoring to shore.

It definitely feels like time for a well-deserved ice cream cone, but Roche Harbor is still operating in pre-summer mode. At the ice cream stand, workers are making last minute preparations, cutting boards and swinging hammers, not yet ready for business.

"We'll be open tomorrow," says one of the workers.

Figures.

The general store has packaged ice cream, so I select a drumstick and Margy goes for a nut-covered strawberry bar. We sit on the bench outside the store, watching workers zipping back and forth, pulling two-wheeled carts full of construction materials and supplies for the tent vendors who will soon make their temporary home on the walkway near the hotel.

We're nearly out of time, Margy is exhausted, and I'm feeling lazy. Margy phones for a taxi, telling the dispatcher: "Two tired bike riders and their bikes."

"Happens all the time here," says the dispatcher.

We finish our ice cream while we await the van from San Juan Taxi. The sun slips low enough in the west that there is a hint of coolness, and it's well appreciated. Off-season travel in the Pacific Northwest is a joy. Missing the crowds of summer is not a problem.

◊ ◊ ◊ ◊ ◊ ◊ ◊

Chapter 13

North to Alaska

The dream of many private pilots is to fly to Alaska. Even when based in Los Angeles, it was one of my flying goals. But the challenges for such a trip are significant.

First, there is the distance – just getting to the Canadian border from Los Angeles involves 10 hours of flight time in my Arrow. Then there is the terrain, which is reasonably challenging for a small aircraft. Finally, the weather must be considered.

Summer is the obvious choice of seasons, with long days for flying and sightseeing, comfortable temperatures, and the best flight conditions. But summer weather in the far northern latitudes adds its own peculiar perils. The jet stream (more properly called the polar jet stream) moves north in the summer, marking the battle line between polar and tropical air. In summer, it typically lingers near the Arctic Circle, where it can cause havoc. Storms follow the winding route of the jet stream, so getting to Alaska in the summer involves crossing this storm track.

Then there's the other jet stream – the arctic jet stream, where polar air meets the even-colder arctic air mass. This high-latitude jet stream seldom makes it very far south, even in winter. In summer, it typically lies above the Arctic Circle, but occasionally it moves far enough south to affect a flight to Alaska. Sometimes it merges with the polar jet, creating even more problems.

Combining the challenges of high terrain and stormy weather, any flight from southern BC to Alaska can be unexpectedly interrupted. Flights under instrument flight rules don't solve the problem, since the mountains require high minimum enroute altitudes (MEAs), often well above the ceiling of my Arrow. Additionally, the most common summer weather limitation in this region is the convective airflow associated with thunderstorms, best avoided by flying VFR rather than

IFR. Flying outside the clouds allows a better lookout for scattered thunderstorms.

Thus, it is not surprising that my plans to fly to Alaska have been thwarted on several occasions. Fortunately, there's a lot to see in northern Canada, even if you don't make it across the Alaskan border. In small aircraft, flexibility counts.

On one successful trip into Alaska, our flight entered Canada at Abbottsford. Then it was north to Prince George for fuel. From there, the weather forecast looked marginally acceptable. Daytime convection was expected to increase as the day progressed, cumulus clouds building under warm, clear skies with an afternoon shift towards instability. The forecast for our destination, Watson Lake (Yukon), included scattered thunderstorms late in the day. Considering the high MEAs and the possibility of thunderstorms, IFR was not worth consideration. It seemed reasonable to attempt the route on a VFR flight plan, with the option of diverting east to Fort St. John or back to Prince George, if weather conditions went downhill fast.

The route from Prince George to Watson Lake follows a geographic anomaly called the Trench, a 400-mile-long valley gouged through northern British Columbia by ancient glaciers. The Trench leads through Williston Lake, which sits between high ridges of the northernmost part of the Canadian Rockies. The alternate flight route north follows the Alaska (Alcan) Highway from Fort Saint John to Watson Lake. Thus, almost all flights in this region converge at Watson Lake, then proceed on to Whitehorse and into Alaska.

Leaving Prince George, we climb under clear skies to our cruising altitude of 8,500 feet, high enough to clear the mountain peaks along the route and a good vantage point from which we can detect any towering cumulus clouds that could develop into thunderstorms. When a few clouds begin to pop up around us (no surprise), we climb to 10,500, which is as high as I normally feel comfortable flying in the Arrow. At this altitude, aircraft performance is noticeably reduced, and oxygen deprivation can begin to take its toll.

We monitor the local Flight Service frequency, keeping track of the weather at Watson Lake. Occasional rain showers are now crossing the airport, and the surface winds are gusty, but there is no reason to alter our course yet. Our flight progress is hampered by the winds aloft, which are strong off our nose, but Margy is an expert at monitoring fuel consumption, duration, and range. She reports all is okay with our fuel reserves, but we'll need to keep a close eye on the ever-changing weather situation.

When the scattered clouds merge into a broken layer of cumulus, I initiate a climb even higher, leveling off at 12,500 feet. This is acceptable for a few minutes, but it's not an altitude I prefer to maintain. For now, it solves the problem of broken cumulus clouds, which are better flown over than under, if you want to avoid turbulence. The headwinds are even stronger at this altitude, but there are still plenty of opportunities to slip down between the clouds.

Finally, Watson Lake is in sight through the broken layer, and we begin our descent. We slip onto final approach and safely down and over the lake to a landing on the comfortable 5000-foot-long paved runway. We'll be camping here for the night, but we elect to get fuel first, so we'll be ready to depart early in the morning.

While we taxi towards the small terminal building, a rain shower passes over the airport. When we pull up in front of the terminal, it begins to pour. In fact, the rain is so heavy that it completely obliterates the building in front of us. This is nicely timed with engine shutdown, so rather than exit the airplane, we elect to sit inside for a few minutes and let the shower dissipate.

As I sit inside the airplane, I feel water dripping in through the overhead door latch. It's not much of an opening, but enough to allow the pounding rain to drip onto my head. After a four-hour flight from Prince George, I'm confined to my seat within a few metres of the terminal building, getting soaked while sitting inside the Arrow.

Just as fast as it started, the rain stops, the sun comes out, and it's a beautiful day in Watson Lake. After refueling, we set up our tent under fair weather cumulus clouds that sweep swiftly past, following the jet stream.

* * * * *

The next morning, we decide to take a breather and stay an extra day at Watson Lake. The weather is adequate to proceed with our trip, but it has rained during the night, and the tent is wet. Rather than pack up under these conditions, it's an easy decision to spend some time playing tourist while we're here.

This is one of my first visits to the interior of British Columbia, and I'm thrilled when I take a swim in the lake and encounter my first loon. It's quite a ways down the shore, so far that I can't even see it, but the cry is definitely the mournful wail of a loon. Surely, I must be in the great white north of Canada. (Later, I learn that loons are found all along the BC coast.)

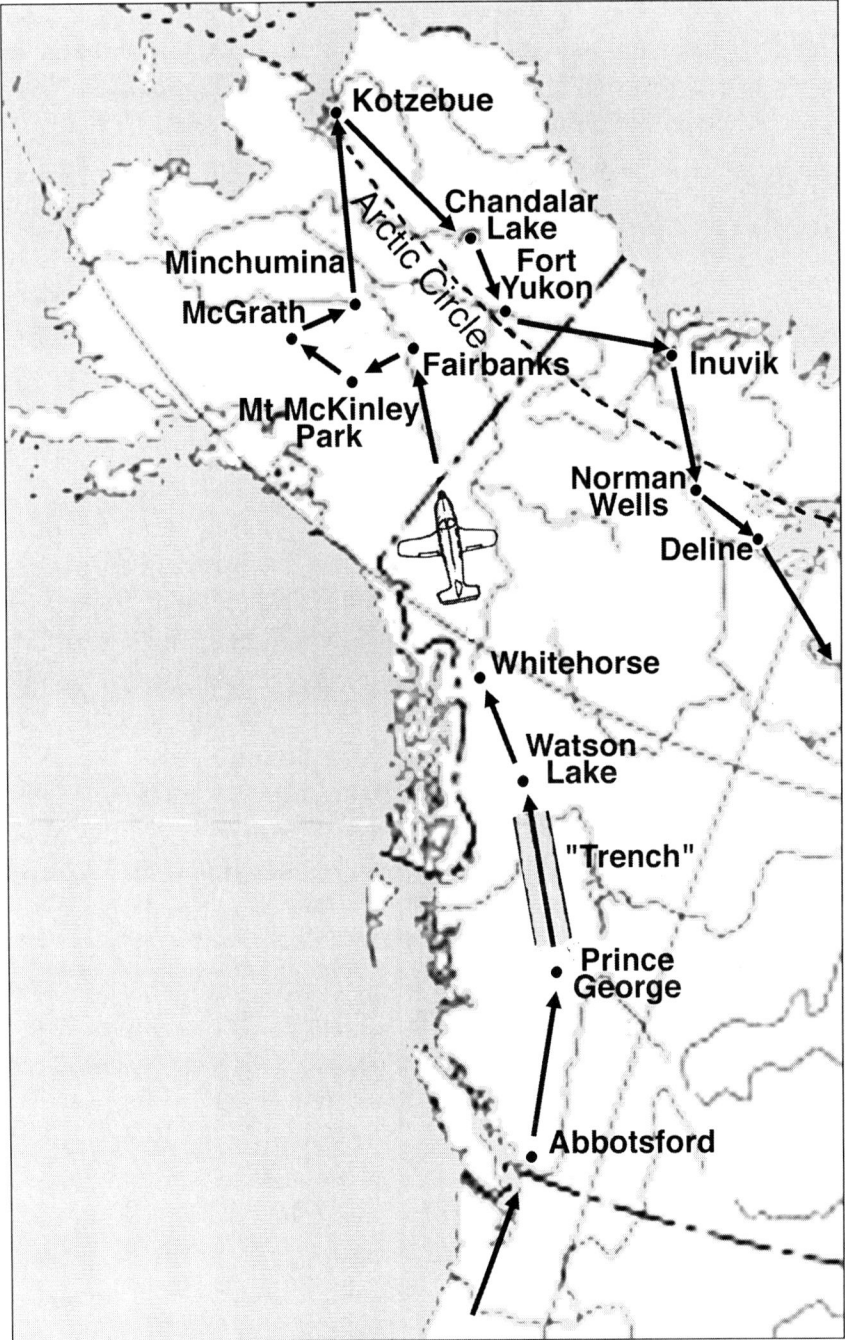

North to Alaska

In town, we use our tourist status to the maximum, visiting the Sign Post Forest and strolling around the gift shops. Margy and I even decide to see a movie, a rare activity for us. We select *Independence Day*, the science fiction film, and it turns out to be a particularly good choice. We sit in the darkened theatre – two Americans among a crowd of Canadians – watching a film about aliens attacking the States. In one dramatic scene, an intense laser beam from space blasts the White House. The crowd bursts into cheers. Suddenly, we realize where we are, and it makes us laugh.

* * * * *

The next morning, our engine suffers a malady commonly called "morning sickness." In just a few seconds, the rough start settles down to a smooth purr, but it's an indication of a sticking valve. I'm able to use the cylinder head temperature (CHT) gauge to diagnose the problem in cylinder number two before the engine smooths out. This information will be helpful if we need to seek maintenance assistance on this trip. For now, the hiccup of morning sickness, unless repeated, is not a no-go situation. The condition is common for high-time Lycoming engines, but it will bear close monitoring. Fortunately, my four-cylinder CHT gauge will be able to assist in keeping track of the startup temperatures associated with this condition.

After leveling off at 8000 feet, now past the highest mountains, we cruise IFR to Whitehorse, then into Alaska. We over-fly Northway, a popular spot for clearing U.S. Customs when entering Canada, planning to fly nonstop to Fairbanks. The weather conditions worsen as the flight progresses, but flying inside the clouds is not a problem under today's stable conditions.

At Fairbanks, we descend on the ILS approach to Runway One-Left, breaking out of the clouds on short final. We land and taxi to the Customs ramp in a gentle rain shower, finally making our way to the camping area on the field. It's a nice overnight spot where two other pilots huddle around a pot-bellied wood stove under a picnic shelter. We join them in the camping area, where we gather around the warmth of the stove for the next three days.

The rain doesn't let up. Conditions are not severe, but low clouds and reduced visibility make it seem like this will last forever. The temperature is cool enough to require a jacket, but it's not cold. The wood stove becomes the meeting place for endless war stories about flying.

One of the pilots (who we respectfully call the "Ol' Guy") is a self-proclaimed aging Piper Cub pilot who is on the solo trip of his dreams. He is about to surrender his pilot certificate for medical reasons, but first he has decided to fly the Trench to Alaska. Now he sits around the fire with us, waiting for weather good enough to continue his journey. The other pilot, although possessing more flight experience than the Ol' Guy, is not instrument rated. So neither of our new friends will be able to depart until the weather improves significantly. Being instrument rated, we could leave at any time, but there are few places to go. The routes to most remote destinations are closed to us by this recent convergence of the polar and arctic jet streams.

The weather at Fairbanks doesn't change, so we keep stoking the fire and telling tales. Eventually, nearby airports, including our desired destination in the national park near Mount McKinley, begin to report clearing skies. When you are in the rain this long, it seems that no place nearby can be sunny. But we finally believe the weather reports and file an IFR flight plan for McKinley.

We depart on Runway One-Niner-Right, and by the time we are 20 miles south, we break above the clouds while climbing to our cruising altitude of 7000 feet. This is our first view of the sun for four days, and the cockpit seems vibrant in the bright rays. Below us, the clouds begin to dissipate as we continue south, until we find ourselves cruising in partly cloudy skies as we approach McKinley Park Airport.

After camping overnight at the national park, we depart for a photo flight around Mount McKinley (Denali), climbing above a low layer of stratus. The mountain pokes through into the rich blue sky, with wisps of windswept clouds surrounding the top.

We land at McGrath (population 415), a town that depends on airplanes to move its people and supplies. The airport's Miner's Cave cafe is a nice place for lunch, and provides us with a good place to observe the local mood. There are no road connections into the town except winter trails, enhancing the island-like atmosphere and the feeling of remoteness.

I'd like to do some fishing while we are in Alaska, and I've packed fresh-water fishing gear, but I'll need a license. Surely this town has a store where I can purchase one.

A Miner's Cave customer helps us find the place. But it isn't a store. Like many of the small businesses in town, you buy your fishing license at a local resident's house. We walk down the road, past several homes where sled dogs bark at us from their kennels. Finally, we come to a sign that reads *Licences*, and I knock on the door. An elderly bearded man, who I imagine to be a retired miner or trapper, invites us into his kitchen. Within a few minutes, I'm licensed to fish in Alaska and have purchased a "super lure" guaranteed to catch northern pike.

From McGrath, we fly to Minchumina Lake, where we land on a 4200-foot gravel strip at the edge of the water. A Piper Cub with oversized tundra tires is the only other airplane parked at the camping area, so we give the plane lots of privacy as we select another spot to set up our tent.

Margy hikes around the shoreline, finding interesting chunks of beaver wood, while I try out my new fishing lure. I wade into the lake at the weedy shore, until I am positioned perfectly and able to cast into the deeper water. Almost immediately, I catch a northern pike (super lure!), its powerful body fighting me all the way in. In a few more minutes, I catch another pike. It's more than we need for dinner, so I release the second fish.

That evening, we cook the pike over the campfire. It makes a tasty (though bone-filled) meal. Darkness approaches, but never seems to arrive. Finally, we give into the lingering twilight and climb into our tent, to sleep on the edge of a beautiful Alaskan lake, surrounded by scenery that rivals the finest national parks.

* * * * *

The next day, after a flight north to Kotzebue just to log crossing the Arctic Circle (although barely), we begin our return trip across Alaska, east towards the Yukon. But first we stop overnight at Chandalar Lake, 60 miles above the Arctic Circle. The 3000-foot gravel runway at an elevation of 1920 feet is barely within our limits, considering our gross weight, but the Arrow handles it well. The airport sits on the edge of the lake, and we feel comfortable with a wide runway clear-zone across the lake.

A derelict Cessna, apparently abandoned, sits off the side of the runway. Three 55-gallon drums of fuel are cached nearby. I pound on the side of the drums – they are full. It seems irreverent to poke into someone else's business, so I leave the airplane alone and climb down the small cliff at the end of the runway to fish.

It's a beautiful July evening, and I catch another northern pike, this time more than big enough for a meal for two. At our makeshift camping spot, we cook the fish over an open grill that someone has constructed from rocks and a metal grate. For two nights in a row, at different lakes in Alaska, we experience the sublime feel of the region. Like most challenges in life, flying north to Alaska pays high personal dividends – warm, intense memories so common when traveling off-the-grid.

◊ ◊ ◊ ◊ ◊ ◊ ◊

Epilogue

The View from Aloft

There is beauty everywhere. There are few places I've visited without values that would draw me back. (Well, okay, except for Fortuna in northern California, but I'm sure it was partly because of that long hike down from the airport on a hot July day.) When my Canadian acquaintances learn I am from Los Angeles, they gasp noticeably. Surely, I must be relieved to finally be away from that city. But Los Angeles is an exciting place, in an entirely different way than Powell River. There is beauty everywhere.

With the unique empowerment of piloting a private aircraft, I've been fortunate to visit wonderful, remote places, as well as the biggest cities. There are places, particularly in the far north, which can only be reached by airplane. I kid my friends that I have seen more of Canada than most Canadians. And it is true – I've camped on the Arctic Ocean, flown over Hudson Bay, and tracked musk oxen on Victoria Island.

I often banter that I discovered Powell River by mistake, and that's basically true. My thirsty Piper Arrow needed gas. From the air, the most obvious landmark was the unappealing tall smokestack of the paper mill. I viewed my first visit as nothing more than a fuel stop. Then I'd be on my way for bigger and better adventures. Yet, here I am, still in Powell River for almost a decade, after having traveled to some of the most beautiful places on earth.

From the air (or boat, or choose your mode of transportation), coastal British Columbia is a supernatural place. Flying often defies geography that is too easily crossed by an airplane. In my Piper Arrow, I can fly from Powell River to Bute Inlet in less than an hour. Try that same trip in a boat (it's a trip that is impossible by car). As beautiful as the aerial view of Bute might be on a sunny day, the all-day trip by sea is unequalled. To really see these mountains where they drop into the sea, you must be on the water.

When I fly over an urban area, picking out the stores and industrial plants, I often stare momentarily at a factory (one eye on the instruments and the other searching for conflicting traffic, of course). I wonder about those who work down there. What a deep appreciation I have for being up here, looking down on those factories. But there are other places equally lofty – looking up at the mountains of Bute Inlet from a boat, or across at Goat Island from my float cabin on Powell Lake.

Beauty is everywhere. And it's all in the eyes of the beholder.

◊ ◊ ◊ ◊ ◊ ◊ ◊

Appendix A
Cockpit Instruments and Avionics

N41997 Cockpit -- 1974 Piper Arrow II

ADF (top) and Northstar GPS-LORAN (bottom)

DME (top-right); VOR (bottom-right) shows slightly off-course; Flight Director with annunciator panel (below DME) and command bars (top left); HSI (bottom-left) shows on-course indication

Throttle Quadrant: throttle (left-black); prop control (center-blue); mixture control (right-red). CHT-EGT gauge at right.

Horizontal Situation Indicator (HSI) during Instrument Landing System (ILS) approach. Aircraft is intercepting the course from the left, and nearly on glide slope ("bugs" to left and right side)

Garmin GPS (GNS 430) with Audio Panel (above)

CHT/EGT Gauge: currently monitoring cylinder #1 for cylinder head temperature and exhaust gas temperature

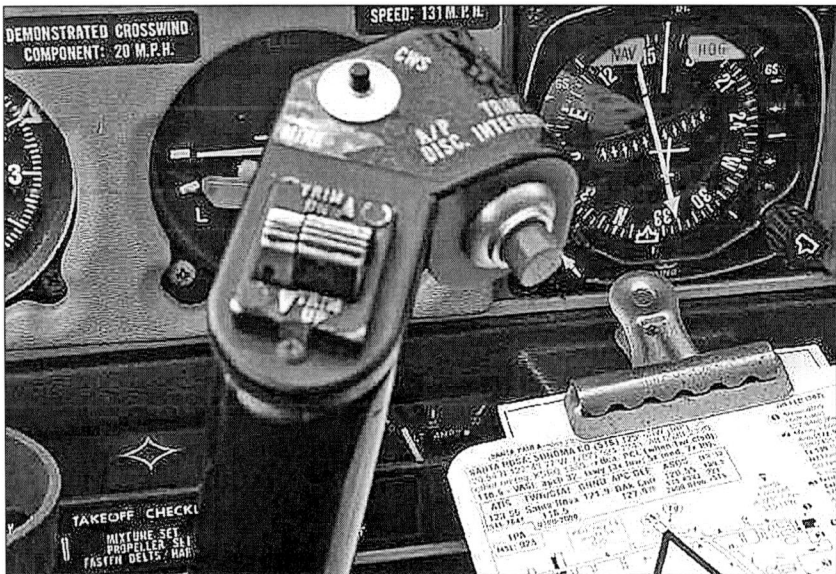

Pilot's Yoke: autopilot disconnect button (right); electric pitch trim (split switch); CWS (control wheel steering to override autopilot)

Manifold Pressure (top-left, controlled by throttle); Fuel Flow (bottom-left, controlled by mixture lever); RPM (right, controlled by prop lever); landing gear down-and-locked lights (green) below gear extension handle

Transponder with standard VFR squawk (beacon) code of 1200

Appendix B

Aviation Terminology and Abbreviations

Alpha Route (Amber Route); e.g., A16 – Canadian airways based on NDBs; no such navigation routes exist in the U.S. today.

Air Route Traffic Control Center or "Center" (ARTCC) – ATC facilities that cover altitudes above and between Approach Control (above and between Terminal Control in Canada).

Air Traffic Control (ATC) – Nav Canada controllers or Federal Aviation Administration (FAA) specialists in the U.S.

Approach Control – ATC facility, usually radar equipped, for assisting pilots during approach and departure; called "Terminal Control" in Canada.

Automatic Direction Finder (ADF) – navigational indicator that allows tracking to-from non-directional beacons (NDBs).

Common Traffic Advisory Frequency (CTAF) – the primary frequency for radio communication at an airport. In Canada, if no other frequency is available, pilots use 126.7 MHz.

Community Aerodrome Radio Station (CARS) – facilities in remote regions that handle local air traffic and relay information from pilots to ATC, particularly for IFR flights.

Cylinder Head Temperature (CHT) – a direct indication of engine overheat condition; particularly important during climb.

Density Altitude – mathematical computation of the thinness of the air, as perceived by an airfoil, due to temperature, pressure, humidity, and actual altitude; e.g. density altitude may be 5000 feet at a sea level airport on a hot, humid, low pressure day.

Distance Measuring Equipment (DME) – provides digital reading of distance to a VOR or other ground station; not as accurate as GPS distance due to slant range error that increases with altitude.

Exhaust Gas Temperature (EGT) – temperature that provides an indication of proper mixture control; high EGT indicates a mixture that is too lean.

Flight Director (FD) – sophisticated avionics, usually limited to large aircraft, that provide the pilot with additional navigational and attitude data; usually used in conjunction with an autopilot.

Flight Itinerary – a Canadian VFR flight plan that covers an extended period of time, usually several days.

Flight Note (or Flight Notification) – abbreviated VFR flight plan that is filed with a private individual or company, rather than Nav Canada; serves as an alternative to a formal VFR flight plan.

Flight Plan – Nav Canada or FAA filed information for a VFR or IFR flight. Pilots provide information in accordance with a specific list of data proposed for a specific flight.

Flight Service Station (FSS) – Nav Canada or FAA facility that provides preflight weather briefings and in-flight information to pilots; this service is not ATC, but can relay information to ATC.

Fuel Flow Gauge – used for initial leaning of the fuel-air mixture, in conjunction with EGT gauge; indicator calibrated in gallons/hour.

Global Positioning System (GPS) – alternate navigation system, replacing common VOR airways and instrument approaches; not all aviation GPS units are certified for IFR.

Instrument Flight Rules (IFR) – operation in accordance with standards that allow flight in almost any weather conditions; requires special pilot certification, equipment, and flight planning procedures.

Instrument Landing System (ILS) – a precision approach system available at major airports that allows aircraft to land when cloud heights are as low as 200 feet and during low visibilities.

Long Range Navigation (LORAN) – an older area navigation system adopted from marine use. LORAN-C, the current format, has generally been replaced by GPS, and is projected for decommissioning by 2010.

Magneto – Standard ignition source for small airplanes; a self-contained ignition source for the spark plugs that is independent of the battery or alternator; dual magnetos (which are standard) provide redundancy.

Manifold Pressure (MP) – an indicator of engine power, measured in inches of Mercury; this gauge is provided on engines with constant-speed propellers; increased throttle position provides increased manifold pressure.

Minimum Enroute Altitude (MEA) – IFR minimum altitudes that provide terrain clearance and assure VOR or NDB reception on airways.

Mixture Control – cockpit lever that allows adjustment of the fuel-air mixture; engines are leaned for operation at higher altitudes.

Multicom – common frequency used at airports without any established frequency; in Canada, this frequency is 126.7 MHz; in U.S., it is 122.9 MHz; multicom also refers to air-to-air frequencies between aircraft

Non-directional Beacon (NDB) – navigational beacons used for instrument approaches and (in Canada) for enroute navigation. ADF receivers and indicators are used for NDB navigation.

Prop Control – cockpit lever for adjusting the blade angle of a constant-speed propeller; push forward for less pitch and higher RPM.

Squawk (or Squawk Code) - four-digit code set into a transponder that provides ATC with aircraft identification and altitude.

Terminal (Terminal Control) – ATC facility, usually radar-equipped, that handles aircraft in approach and departure phases of flight or for low-alitude passage through an area.

Transponder – radar beacon transmitter in an aircraft that provides continuous data to ATC, including position information: mode-C transponders provide additional altitude information.

Unicom – a non-ATC radio communication station at small airports that provides non-regulatory information such as wind and advisories regarding known traffic.

VHF Omnidirectional Range (VOR) – common equipment for enroute navigation and many non-precision instrument approaches; this system is gradually being replaced by GPS navigation.

Victor Airway (e.g., V27) – established routes between VORs used by most IFR traffic and many VFR aircraft.

Visual Flight Rules (VFR) – flight by reference to the ground in weather conditions with good visibilities and few clouds.

Waypoint – an electronic checkpoint location used in GPS navigation; sometimes called "phantom stations" since they are not dependent upon the location of VORs and NDBs.

About the Author

From 1980 to 2005, Wayne Lutz was Chairman of the Aeronautics Department at Mount San Antonio College in Los Angeles. He led the college's Flying Team to championships as Top Community College in the United States seven times. He has also served 20 years as a U.S. Air Force C-130 aircraft maintenance officer. His educational background includes a B.S. degree in physics from the University of Buffalo and an M.S. in systems management from the University of Southern California.

The author is a flight instructor with 7000 hours of flying experience. For the past three decades, he has spent summers in Canada, exploring remote regions in his Piper Arrow, camping next to his airplane. The author resides in a floating cabin on Canada's Powell Lake and in a city-folk condo in Los Angeles. His writing genres include regional Canadian publications and science fiction. The author's next book, *Farther Up the Lake,* is scheduled for publication in June 2008.

Up the Lake
Up the Main
Up the Winter Trail
Up the Strait
Up the Airway
Farther Up the Lake

Order books and Photo CDs at:
www.PowellRiverBooks.com

Free Audio Chapters for the first 5 books
in this series are now available at the
Powell River Books web site

Reader's can email the author at:
wlutz@mtsac.edu

Blog — http://PowellRiverBooks.blogspot.com

Up the Airway is the 5th in a series of volumes
focusing on the unique places and memorable
people of coastal British Columbia

Up the Lake
Coastal British Columbia Stories

Wayne J. Lutz

Books & Photo CDs

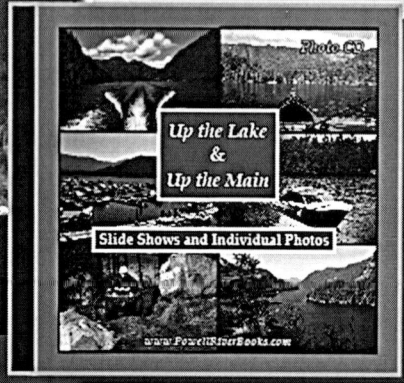

Up the Lake & Up the Main
Slide Shows and Individual Photos
www.PowellRiverBooks.com

Order at: www.PowellRiverBooks.com

$5 Instant Rebate

◊ This offer pertains to all books in this series

◊ Rebate applies to books purchased at the Powell River Books web site – not applicable to in-store retail sales

Rebate details available at:
http://www.PowellRiverBooks.com/rebate.html